CW00507499

HOW TO TURN A MARRIAGE INTO A
LIVING PARADISE

Marriage is easy! Wishing you
a glorious marital life!

Rex Akpojaro

REX AKPOJARO

HOW TO TURN A
MARRIAGE INTO A
LIVING PARADISE

From Difficulty to Marital Bliss

Unless otherwise stated, all scriptures are taken from the *King James Version* of the bible.

Scripture quotations taken from the New American Standard Bible (NASB),
Copyright © 1960, 1962, 1963, 1968, 1971, 1972, 1973, 1975, 1977, 1995 by The Lockman Foundation
Used by permission. www.Lockman.org

HOW TO TURN A MARRIAGE INTO A LIVING PARADISE

From Difficulty to Marital Bliss

ISBN: 978 - 0 - 9954903 - 0 - 7

Copyright © 2016 by Rex Akpojaro

Published by:

Higher Life Publishing

London

Printed in London by: All rights reserved under International Copyright Law. Contents and/or cover may not be reproduced in whole or in part without the express written consent of the publisher.

DEDICATION

*This book is dedicated to my lovely wife, Erhi Akpojaro
who has been by my side for the last 10yrs and patiently
and consistently prayed for our marriage!*

PREFACE

In our society today, marriage has become a very challenging aspect of a majority of married people's individual lives. Not only is this manifested in the ever increasing divorce rates across the nations of the world, but also in the level of unhappiness being experienced in relationships.

A great deal of people are hurting silently, both men and women, due to the inability to unravel this mystery, called marriage! Across the world, you find people who are struggling to cope and trying to work out their marriages which leaves them completely drained.

There are questions that plague the hearts of men and women such as:

Why did God even introduce the institution of marriage?

Why does marriage seem to be such hard work that leaves one exhausted?

Why is that all I do never seems to be enough?

Is this how we are going to be living for the rest of our lives?

Why can't we just be able to get along?

Is there any happiness in marriage?

These and many other questions keep many in a vicious circle of trying and never really finding the happiness they so long for. These are questions whose answers can only be found in the realm of divine wisdom! Until one is illuminated with insight and understanding, there is bound to be difficulty just as in the case of trying to work in the dark.

This book will explore the depths of marital wisdom to unravel this institution of marriage in order to arrive at the place where marriage becomes be the best thing that ever happened to you! This book will approach the subject of marital paradise more from an angle of an expression of an inward reality as opposed to exerting external effort in finding true happiness in your marriage.

We are used to being told what needs doing when it comes to marriage, only to find out that, all our doings, do nothing but to tire us out and are futile in nature. Seeing that we are not human doings but human beings, the only thing we can do effectively is to live as an expression of what we have inside.

Marital paradise is something we must have within us before we can experience it outwardly. As our minds are renewed concerning the beauty and blessing of marriage and all that it makes available to us without any effort, we will come to a place where we live daily in unrestrained and undisturbed happiness and peace.

In this book, we take marriage as a gift of priceless value that only needs to be maintained with minimal effort. It is easier to enjoy a gift than to try and re-create it or add to it, it just needs to be maintained.

The objective of this book is to completely revolutionise one's thinking and mindset towards marriage through wisdom and in turn change the marital experience. It attempts to give an accurate picture of what marriage really is and how spouses can fully transition from a place of difficulty to a living paradise!

CONTENTS

CHAPTER 1
A Culture of Unending Happiness

When we think of marriage, there are three ways we can approach this important aspect of life; What it is meant to be, what it is now and what it is certainly not supposed to be. All three states of marriage are present day realities that can be experienced. It is also possible to move from one reality to another based on our mindset and frame of mind or thinking.

The million dollar question is this; How do we move from one reality to another? How can we move from what marriage is not supposed to be to what it is supposed to be? The golden key that grants you access is divine wisdom! Wisdom is the key that unlocks the doors to higher dimension of life. Wisdom will promote you and bring honour. Wisdom unravels difficulties and makes complex problems easy to resolve.

This book is based entirely on the wisdom that unlocks the door into what I call marital paradise. I am talking about effortless happiness and joy in your marriage from day to day as it should be.

The next big question in the minds of couples is this; How

do we sustain the happiness in our marriage and not end up like others? The secret to keeping your marriage in a continuous state of happiness is this thing called "culture". Just as every geographical region bows its knees to a certain culture that defines them so does the territory of marital paradise submit to the power of a culture!

So what is culture? To help understand and fully harness the richness of culture as it relates to marital happiness, we will use a few definitions.

The Merriam-Webster's Learner's Dictionary defines culture as:

"a way of thinking, behaving, or working that exists in a place or organization".

(Source: Merriam-Webster's Learner's Dictionary)

The Business Dictionary defines Culture this way: "It is a pattern of responses discovered, developed, or invented during the group's history of handling problems which arise from interactions among its members, and between them and their environment. These responses are considered the correct way to perceive, feel, think, and act, and are passed on to the new members through immersion and teaching. Culture determines what is acceptable or unacceptable, important or unimportant, right or wrong, workable or unworkable".

(Source: http://www.businessdictionary.com/definition/culture.html)

From the definitions above we pick out a few things about culture:

One of the key things about culture is that it can be learned and is transferable. It is constituted of wisdom that is from discovery, invention or developed.

It defines interactions, problem resolution, ways of thinking and even how to feel about things. From the above, it becomes clear that the culture of marital happiness can not only be a reality but actually communicated through us to whoever we choose to teach. This culture can be strongly established and entrenched to the point where marital difficulty becomes an impossibility to us. We can become so conditioned to the culture of marital happiness that we know other way than to live in blissful marriages.

This culture teaches us what is acceptable and what is not, how to view and handle challenges, how to respond and how not to, what is important and what isn't in our marriages. This culture can be made to be the only way we know marriage, not by denying obvious contradictory realities on the ground but dealing with them in a way that keeps our happiness intact.

Marital happiness is the culture of marital paradise, and this culture like every other culture can be entered into and learned. It can be studied and completely gotten hold of. It is the only way marriage can be enjoyed and not endured. It is the prescription of highly successful married lives.

It is easier to live through culture than to try to live any other way, hence the power of culture. It is almost impossible to live in a way that is foreign to you as a person and the dominant culture you have embraced. This the root of most marital difficulties, the impossibility of experiencing happiness which belongs to a place that can only be accessed by wisdom.

It is like trying to live and experience things that are inconsistent to the culture you are currently entrenched in. Until there is the learning of a new culture, the experiences of this new culture will be out of reach.

To get the best out of this book, get ready to have your mind challenged and your thinking renewed. Through minor changes in your thinking and mindset, in the mental realm, great changes in your marital life in the physical realm are bound to occur.

CHAPTER 2
A Description of Marital Paradise

The marriage relationship was designed by God to be a heaven-on-earth experience. It is when it is working in the way it was designed to be that it produces a joy in you that words cannot describe. I am speaking about a feeling of happiness that is not dependent on any particular good deed or action from your spouse, it flows constantly.

You start living in an atmosphere-driven state of joy as opposed to actions-driven feelings of happiness. An actions-driven state of happiness is in itself very unstable and can never be sustained in the long term. The other person tires out at some point and whenever these actions are not there, one slumps into a state of disappointment.

A great marriage creates that atmosphere where even the most difficult of circumstances or mistakes by the other partner are easily disarmed of anger and bitterness. Little offences fail to turn into huge mountains and little issues find an atmosphere that makes it impossible for them to grow and fester. There is easy and quick resolution to difficulties and differences that may arise.

Life generally becomes easy since your marriage is a significant aspect of one's life. The presence of this joy characterises the lives of the couple and begins to exude out of them towards every aspect of their lives. It becomes evident in their health, the emotional wellbeing of the children, their relationships with others and their general outlook on life.

Marriage is truly a blessing from God and the joy of it is limitless!

Marriage should enrich you.

If we are of the belief that marriage is a blessing and not a curse, then there are certain attributes of a blessing that should be manifested in our marriages.

The very first thing that our marriage should be to us is something that enriches our lives and not be the object of stress. A blessing enriches and comes with no sorrows. When you think of your marriage, it ought to produce feelings of joy and peace within you. There ought to be good feelings about life emanating from the fact that you are in a wonderful relationship called marriage.

Secondly, your marriage should be working for you and not the other way round. A marriage you constantly have to prop up and labour for, is in reality, a curse. You do not buy flowers and lingerie or gift after gift for him or her to love you. Why? Simply because at some point you will run out of steam. You will also find that you never really had anything close to a blessing but a self-generated and self-sustained marital prison. You do these good things **because** you have a great marriage and not the other way round. The nature of a cursed life is hard labour and sweat while a blessed life is rest and enjoyment. Your marriage should work for you by adding to what you already are and have and increasing your worth in life. It should be working for your health and producing joy and happiness that keeps you physically and emotionally healthy. It is the objective of this book to bring folks to a place where mindsets are changed concerning marriage and each one is able to say with every confidence – "my marriage is a blessing!"

Thirdly, your marriage as a blessing should empower you and give you the added advantage that you would not otherwise have had on your own. The purpose of a blessing is to empower you beyond the physical limits to enjoy the benefits of a supernatural position. A blessing makes you enjoy benefits that you would otherwise not have qualified for. You ought not to be dissipating your strength, straining yourself and labouring to make things work. Your marriage ought to strengthen you to the point that you are able to confront and tackle and overcome the daily challenges that life throws at you!

You may ask, does such a state of marriage really exist? The answer is "yes" and it is within your reach.

The moment by moment feeling of satisfaction and contentment

Marriage is what the average person looks forward to as the crowning moment of life. Women look to the joy of being in a stable relationship, the permanence of companionship and the security of being loved and cherished by a husband. She also sees this as the seal of her status amongst women in society. This is the pinnacle of her dreams, having a beautiful home and family and a wonderful life. With this in mind, one would and should expect that this is what they will find in marriage. When this is not the case, the disappointment is monumental, yet this is the situation for many. The reality is that the absolute satisfaction and contentment in marriage is not just a possibility but should be the result of the good marriage you have. It is not something you work for. Rather, it is an output of being married and as one's mind-set is changed, one will find these realities becoming a daily experience.

For men, when the time comes to settle down, the desire for marriage is even stronger than in women. He dreams of a home where he can find rest and raise a family and leave a legacy. He dreams of a home where the leader in him will come forth and he can be respected and treated as the king that he is. He sees marriage as a place where he can find peace and rest from the daily assault of life that he faces when he goes out to make a living.

When he gets into marriage and he is confronted with daily issues from his wife, he can begin to experience feelings of regret. This is the case even though he knows in his heart that getting married to the wife he chose was the right decision at the time and a well thought out one. As a man, in your marriage, you can wake up every day with a big grin on your face fully satisfied with the wife you have. You can come to a place where on a daily basis, you express gratitude to God for blessing you with such a person as your spouse. The satisfaction that I speak of here is so powerful that it is what will neutralise any lust in you for other women.

The joy of companionship

As God said in His word, "*it is not good for the man to be alone*" (Gen 2:18). Humanity was built for companionship. It is amazing how many couples experience loneliness in their marriage.

A marriage that is functioning the way it should, generates for you an amazing experience of companionship. It is the joy of having someone to live life with, enjoy good times with, face challenging times with, travel with and grow old with. Achievements and successes that are not shared become the very object of emptiness and worthlessness. You increase and achieve together and share individual achievements. You share your fears and draw comfort from each other and it gives a certain richness to your life. You deal with things together and you give each other the courage to tackle life's challenges. This is what you should expect and will experience by the time you put this book down and begin to change your mind-set about your current marriage. You truly can have a new marriage with the very same partner you are with.

The feeling of emotional wellbeing

Emotional health is a very important aspect of human life. As a matter of fact, physical health in many cases is linked to emotional wellbeing. Due to the fact that marriage brings us all to a place of emotional vulnerability, a lot of married couples find their marriages to be the greatest source of pain and hurt.

A marriage that is working will produce emotional wellness within you and cause you to be at peace with yourself and your spouse. When you are emotionally whole, you are in a position to love and be loved, to accurately judge people and competently deal with the issues of life. You maintain a certain level of rationality as you are not dealing with things from a place of hurt and pain. You are able to enjoy your spouse and allow them to be themselves as you are able to correctly discern their intentions without jumping to conclusions.

The ability to resolve differences without any emotional wounds

The majority of the big issues that build up and eventually wreck marriages usually start as small differences that fester and grow into mountains. A healthy marriage is one in which an atmosphere exists where even if hurtful things are mistakenly done to a spouse, they are never translated into emotional wounds that linger on and turn into deep-seated hurts.

What you have instead, is an environment where negativity finds it difficult to survive. Difficulties easily find resolution with little effort. In situations where a compromise cannot be reached on issues, this is successfully isolated from the overall marriage and dealt with at a future time. The atmosphere that exists just cannot allow for the survival or growth of emotional cancers of bitterness, regret, pain and wounds.

This gives you the confidence to express yourself without walking on egg shells.

The satisfaction of being understood

There is nothing as frustrating as not being understood. It breeds resentment and is the fire that fuels most arguments. A healthy marriage deals with those issues of the heart and mind that make us misunderstand our spouses. Issues that are unresolved are the very tools that make us misinterpret what our spouses are communicating to us. Their messages are obscured by the cloudiness of other issues in the marriage.

A healthy marriage clears the deck and allows you to see things for what they are. You are then able to decipher with ease what is behind what is being said or communicated. To be understood by your spouse is a priceless asset to be treasured.

The unity of thought, purpose and destiny

As the bible says *"Can two walk together except they agree?"* (Amos 3:3). No one can ever put an accurate value on a couple who have become one in thinking, purpose and destination. This is a property of a healthy marriage that makes the married life a living paradise. It creates so much energy and enthusiasm to enjoy the journey of marriage.

While your personalities may be different, your thinking on the key aspects of life are found to be the same. You are on the same wavelength and there is no pulling each other apart and you enjoy little or no friction. You find yourself being united in purpose and this gives meaning and perspective to everything you do for your marriage. When two hearts are beating as one, it makes it easier to advance towards common goals and objectives.

CHAPTER 3

A Difficult Marriage

Maybe you are reading this book at a time when your marriage has become so difficult that you just can't see a way forward and you are at the end of the rope. Not only does your marriage seem so far from what was described in the preceding chapter, you cannot see it ever getting there. Everything seems so hopeless and the emotional pain you live in on a daily basis cannot even be expressed in words. You have either experienced or are currently experiencing some of the symptoms described below and you are at your wits end. It is for such levels of difficulties that this book was written.

Symptoms of a difficult marriage:

1. Regular arguments and conflicts

This is one of the most stressful and difficult characteristics of a troubled marriage. You literally find yourselves arguing over everything and even the smallest of things. The most painful aspect is that even when you set out to express love and do things that should bring some moments of peace and sanity, it turns into a disagreement or at best a heated conversation.

Positions are entrenched and no one sees any reason to give ground. Even attempts to give ground for peace sake still end up in arguments. The couple experience difficulties in finding peace and not a week goes by without an argument or a resignation to just keeping quiet and avoiding each other.

At the root of these constant arguments is anger that is fed by issues that have not been addressed. These unaddressed issues go on to produce more issues and both people are at a loss on how to find peace in the marriage. The best analogy for this is like being trapped in a small cage with an angry tiger.

2. Being constantly misunderstood and communication becoming increasingly stressful.

This is extremely frustrating for couples and painful that the other person is just completely blind to things that are obvious. It even gets worse where you start to feel that you are being deliberately misunderstood by your partner and the more you strongly put forward your case on any issue the more they take it the wrong way. You say "A" and they hear "B" and react according to what they hear and not what you are communicating.

Deep-seated frustration begins to turn into stress and high blood pressure. Communication becomes painful and difficult to the extent that most conversations demand that you first ask yourself if it is worth the stress. Everything is viewed and interpreted from a place of anger and hurt. Simple points that are raised for discussion are misunderstood and taken as an attack.

The third angle to this is that one person's cry for help and resolution is being interpreted as just whining, complaining, being negative and making the marriage unbearable. It leaves the other party living a life of hell on earth. This applies to men and women in the same proportion and can be one of the worst feelings on earth.

Communication in itself is not the problem, but only a manifestation of a deeper problem which is what is responsible for generating all the characteristics of a troubled marriage. Until the "trouble" in the marriage is dealt with, nothing done to fix these issues will have any effect.

3. Feelings of apathy and a loss of interest in your spouse

This is usually as a build-up of frustration over a period of time. You come to a place where you just don't care anymore and you cannot be bothered about your spouse or the relationship. You are so tired and emotionally exhausted from constantly being wounded and hurt, tired of arguments, tired of hearing painful statements and emotionally exhausted from the up and down and the back and forth.

At this stage, you don't even care whether the marriage collapses or survives. You lose interest both in your spouse and the relationship itself. You become indifferent to their existence and you take each day as it comes. You lose all fear of your spouse leaving and start to think of life beyond your current spouse. This is a sentiment you have no problem expressing publicly or to anyone who ventures into asking you about your marriage.

With the state of things in your marriage, you may ask, "with such sentiments, is there really any hope for this marriage? Could this horrible pit I find myself in, ever turn into the so-called living paradise that is spoken of?" It is exactly for these levels of difficulty that the wisdom of this book is meant for.

4. Persistent feeling of stress just thinking about coming back home from work!

Here we are talking about a level of dread one experiences just around the time you need to start making your way home from wherever you may be. Just the thought alone of being at home fills you with the type of stress a person experiences who is just about to be locked in a cage with a hungry and angry tiger.

You live each day with a huge weight on your shoulders and pain in your heart. As you think of the things your spouse does or says, you get even angrier and irate which in turn increases your stress levels.

It isn't long before your body begins to respond to the very high levels of stress. You may find your left eye twitching or some other bodily manifestation of the presence of stress in you. You start operating or living beneath your optimal level of life and there are health problems that are picked up at this place of marital difficulty.

5. A deep sense of loneliness

It is in humanity's very nature to despise loneliness and yet this is the experience of many people in their marriage. In a difficult marriage, it isn't just loneliness that a person experiences but the feeling of "being alone". This is one of the most painful aspects of a broken relationship. Each person has retreated inwards and challenges are no longer faced together. Concerns or fears are no longer shared, successes are kept inside and this becomes a very unbearable experience.

The main form of punishment that is meted out to humans when a crime is committed is imprisonment, a separation from people, a confinement of one to himself. This is so because isolation and loneliness are what man (humanity) was certainly not created for. Even God at the beginning said that it is not good for man to be alone.

One will be amazed at how many marriages exist in this state where there is no true relationship anymore within the marriage. Rather, it is just two people living together, trapped by either their children or societal expectations. You could say at this point that a lot of people are hurting in this world but thank God for His wisdom to undo the most difficult of situations.

6. Sexual intimacy becoming undesirable

Sexual intimacy is a very key aspect of marriage that is supposed to bring closeness, enjoyment, relaxation and pleasure. The sexual act itself is tied to our emotions and for it to be enjoyed and fulfilling for both men and women, there needs to be emotional oneness. It is for this reason that a man can sleep with all the prostitutes in the world and yet find no sexual satisfaction nor fulfilment.

With a marriage in difficulty, there is usually emotional

disequilibrium and division within the heart. The husband and wife are not connected mentally and emotionally which makes physical intimacy to be un-enjoyable, dissatisfying and emotionally draining. To be quite honest, it feels like not being worth it most of the time.

7. You freely criticise your spouse to others rather than covering him/her

As a marriage becomes more and more difficult to be in, criticizing your spouse to anyone who cares to listen becomes a regular occurrence. It becomes the only way you can find relief from what you consider to be the irrational and difficult behaviour of your spouse.

The refusal of your spouse to see reason with you and to come to a common understanding generates so much frustration and pain. This then leads you to look for anyone who can understand your points of view and see reason with you. The more you slay him or her in public, the more relief you feel that, at least, you are not the cause of the problem. This is a very difficult place to be in.

8. You no longer have shared dreams or goals

Difficulties in a marriage get to a point where they start to generate doubts about the future of the marriage and the relationship itself. Spouses become unsure of any future for the marriage and withdraw inwards to protect themselves. Shared dreams and visions quickly evaporate and this is one of the major causes of failure in achieving family goals and objectives - the absence of a supportive spouse.

We were never designed to succeed alone but to connect with our spouse and unleash the greatness that is within us. We fail when we walk alone and this is what a difficult marriage does to our unity of purpose.

9. You stop dating and hanging out

Due to the difficulty in being able to sustain simple conversations without it turning into an argument, it starts to become less appealing to engage in any romantic outings or date nights. To save one's self from any hurt, spouses withdraw into themselves and just do the minimum to maintain a civil relationship. This leads to loneliness, boredom and unhappiness. This is a hellish place to be in for any marriage.

10. Feelings of regret

Regret can be thought of as *a feeling of sadness, or disappointment over an occurrence or something that one has done or failed to do.* In this case, the sadness and pain is over the decision to get married to the person you married. This is the most painful aspect of a difficult marriage. You reflect on the dreams you once had as a young person, a future life of bliss and a flourishing life. Then, you begin to feel like you made the biggest mistake of your life by your choice of marital partner. Regret is a very painful feeling and it is at this point you start to give up any hope for your marriage.

CHAPTER 4

Revolutionary Shift in our View of Marriage

1. The difference between dating and marriage

It is important to have a sound understanding of what marriage is so as to fully realise all the benefits and blessings of it. One of the very surprising phenomena of relationships is a scenario where people enjoy a long term dating relationship spanning several years but then...the second they get married, all hell breaks loose. This turns into the beginning of a living hell or in certain cases the entire relationship breaks down and everyone goes their separate ways.

Dating and marriage are two completely different platforms in which we engage a spouse and they operate under different rules. Courtship is nothing short of a period of getting to know someone if they will be suitable to enter into the institution we know as marriage. One is an institution and the other is not. One has foundations and the other doesn't. It is for these reasons that the rules and principles that govern these two forms of relationship are completely different and it is important that this is understood.

For the benefit of those just getting married and finding your relationship experiencing difficulties and being in a strange place, this is the reason why.

Neither you nor your spouse has changed, but what has happened is that you have been ushered into an institution with its own rules and realities. This is the reason many encounter such difficulties in marriage because they use the mind-set and realities of dating to function in marriage and this leads to problems.

The institution of marriage is God's gift to humanity not just to enjoy but to also bring one into a world of unbelievable happiness and joy. Marriage is an institution of blessings. When a marriage is operating in the dimension that it should operate in, no amount of words can describe the experience of such a happy life. An understanding of the principles and the mind-set that marriage demands of you will bring you into a place where it will unleash on you an out-of-this-world lifetime experience.

An institution consists of structures and mechanisms that enable it to function and achieve its purpose. The good news about marriage as an institution is that it comes with all its structures and mechanisms needed to make it work.

2. Marriage is a favour and a blessing.

Pro 18:22 *He who finds a wife finds a good thing and obtains favour from the LORD.*

The Google online dictionary describes favour as "*an act of kindness beyond what is due or usual*". Marriage is a blessing and, by its very nature, a blessing or favour is something beyond what you can achieve in your own strength and ability. A blessing is something that is far beyond what is due to you or even what you deserve. This means there is nothing you can do to add to it or make it any better because it is beyond you. It is a gift and all that makes it what it is and what it possesses comes along with the gift from the giver. This piece of truth is a major shift from what we have always been taught about marriage.

The normal average mind-set on marriage is based on hard work to make it better, keep it going and do everything we can to make it succeed or survivable. This is the very cause of all the marital difficulty we experience in the world today. The honest truth is that a great deal of people are going through such emotional hurt and difficulty in their marriages that, if they really had the option, they would prefer not to be in the marriage that they are in. The inability to see marriage as a blessing that comes fully loaded causes us to go on a wild goose chase looking for things that we are unaware came with our marriage.

It may be very difficult for us to accept marriage as a blessing because of what we see around us e.g. the high rates of divorce and distress amongst married couples. However, until we are enlightened with the truth, the calamity of walking in darkness can go on for generations. Our general life experiences are a product of our thinking and mind-set. Until there is a fundamental shift in our thinking concerning marriage, we will find no way out of being trapped in the average marriage which is difficult and gets worse by the day.

A blessing is something that is bestowed by the giver but has to be received by the intended recipient and can never be forced on anyone. A blessing is an empowerment to bring into reality what you naturally will not be able to do in your own strength. A blessing is not based on external factors. Instead, it impacts its environment rather than being limited by it. Think of marriage not based on your circumstances or your partner's behaviour but based on the fact that it is a blessing and to be enjoyed

Regardless of how difficult your experiences may have been, a change in mind-set will unleash the full payload of the blessing upon your relationship. You will begin to experience a joy, happiness and satisfaction that is beyond whatever your spouse does to make you happy or unhappy. It is a happiness and joy that is proceeding from an atmosphere that you cannot quite figure out or trace to any one of your efforts or actions.

I believe that marriage is a blessing primarily because the scriptures declare it to be so. Even if you look at humanity across all cultures, regardless of religious beliefs, marriage continues to be the number one aspiration of almost all of humanity and there is a race to get into it. I believe it is the human instinct within that is drawn to the marital institution because it recognises the blessing it brings to human life.

When dealing with truth, we do not start from deviations or contradictions to establish truths. Instead, we seek to analyse all deviations and contradictions in the light of what has been established to be the truth. I say this because we do not look at the marriages around us to draw conclusions about the truth. Rather, we use the truth to change the marriages around us. The day you make a decision to change your mind-set about marriage, that will be the day your world will change in terms of your marriage.

By holding on to your negative experiences as the truth, that will only produce an even more negative marriage. By embracing the truth that your marriage is a blessing, all deviations from the truth will have no option but to align themselves to the truth.

3. Enjoying and not Labouring

Embracing the reality that we come into a blessing when we enter into marriage, we must understand that a gift is not something you work for but something you receive and enjoy. We, as human beings, are ever so imprisoned by this desire to *do* rather than to *be*. After all, we are not human doings but human beings. We always want to fix things and do things and find it difficult to just relax and enjoy the blessings that are bestowed upon us.

Using the analogy of a gift, there is nothing you can do to add to a gift or work for a gift other than just to enjoy it. It is exactly the same with marriage, it is a gift fully loaded with all it needs to provide you with an unbelievable life of happiness. We are fed such lines like "marriage is hard, it requires a lot of work"; "marriage is up and down" and "marriage is not for the faint-hearted". These beliefs create the wrong mind-set which in turn creates a difficult marital life and experience. In the Bible, *labour* is an indication of a cursed life while *rest* is an indication of living under a blessing.

There is nothing you can do to add to the marital blessing other than to enjoy every bit of it, as shocking as this may sound to you. You cannot be constantly working or doing this or that to make your marriage work, or make your spouse happy. It is a difficult and laborious life that is sure to produce nothing and is bound to fail. If a husband should buy all the flowers in the world it will not end the thirst for happiness and he will forever be looking for what to do next.

It is exactly the same for the woman, no matter how many times one changes lingerie to make her husband happy, it will not end the desire for more. The labour and hard work mentality make a marriage all the more thorny and the experience hard. The "marriage is hard work" mentality deprives you of the opportunity to enjoy the marriage. Your main priority should be to rise up every day and see your marriage as blessed, treat it as a blessing and use that mind-set to maintain the atmosphere that keeps the beauty of your marriage intact.

The bulk of the work we do is in trying to change our spouse and, by now, the world has come to understand that this is a futile venture. After all, this is the person we were so excited and happy to marry as they were. Now, we somehow think that we made a terrible mistake and must try and change them. This here is the beginning of our misery. We fail to recognise the blessing in the spouse that we have and the continuous failure to see them as a blessing causes things to get worse in the marriage.

You did not make a mistake in your decision to marry the person you married and this is the truth. Where the issue is, is that marriage exposes personality differences. Conflicts arise when we are faced with differences that clash with the way we do things.

Personality differences can be a huge asset that can be exploited to a couple's advantage through wisdom. It is a strength that can truly benefit your marriage and something you can enjoy. We have no need to change one another but to celebrate our difference and let the blessings of marriage take us from one dimension of splendour to another.

4. The gift comes complete

The truth is that your spouse is a gift to you regardless of the heartaches and stress they may have caused you. The majority of the difficulty that is experienced in marriage is caused by a wrong mind-set. It cannot be overemphasized to state the impact of one's mind-set on their actions, conduct and entire experience in life.

The second you begin to see and embrace your spouse as a blessing rather than an object of regret you will be amazed at the speed with which every pain and hurt will be evacuated from within you. Also, that will be the day you will begin to see changes in behaviour and attitudes within the marriage that are involuntarily generated by a change in the atmosphere. Your mentality exudes the atmosphere which in turn determines what happens in the marriage.

Here we focus on the excellence of the gift you have received from God and, yes, your spouse is a gift from God to you. In your spouse are treasures to be mined out for your benefit. There are treasures and access to higher dimensions of life that are locked up in your partner that are to be discovered by you.

If for one minute your eyes were to be opened to all that your spouse is loaded with and all that you stand to benefit from their presence in your life, your heart will explode with joy.

Based on all the difficult times you may have experienced with your partner, there is just no way right now that this person can be anything but a huge mistake in your eyes. This is something that we will need to change - the view we have of our spouse. A change of view will open your eyes to the good things in them. It will unearth all these treasures that exist in them for you.

You may be surprised to know that your spouse came into your life with all that is needed to bring the best in life out of you. You are to be exhilarated with the love of your spouse and not despondent about their faults. You are to be ecstatic about your spouse and the truth about them - not the facts - for truth never changes but facts are subject to change. It demands that you take your eyes off behavioural and annoying attitudes and put them firmly on the unseen, yet-to-be discovered treasures that lie within.

Let your fountain be blessed, and rejoice in the wife of your youth. As a loving hind and a graceful doe, Let her breasts satisfy you at all times; Be exhilarated always with her love. (Proverbs 5:18-19 NASB version)

A different perspective on Love and Respect

One of the main issues in marriages is the vicious circle of love and respect. The man complains "my wife doesn't respect me and because of that I cannot show any love to her", and the wife complains that "I don't respect my husband because he doesn't love me." This vicious cycle goes on and on and on. The marriage becomes a very bitter experience and there never seems to be any way out of it. Then we start to demand love and respect from the opposite spouse and this now becomes the hard work that we hear about all the time in marriage. The wife starts striving to respect the husband and he tries to love the wife and it doesn't take long before both parties find out that this is impossible to carry out and the marriage gets worse.

The truth is that love and respect are not things we are to see as work in our marriages but instead as responsibilities we have in ensuring an atmosphere that supports the blessing that we have received as marriage.

With every blessing comes a responsibility to maintain that blessing. It is the same as if you gave somebody a car as a gift - they still have a responsibility to maintain the car. No matter how new and expensive it is, it will require maintenance and care. In the same way, once you have received the blessing of marriage, it will require maintenance.

Love and respect should be seen as the things that we do to maintain the blessing we have received. Love and respect ensures that the appropriate atmosphere for you to enjoy the blessing is sustained. It is much easier and more natural for you to love and respect your spouse because you are **in** a happy marriage, not to **achieve** a happy marriage.

Except you embrace your marriage itself as good, no matter what is applied to it you are only building on a defective foundation and will forever be repairing crack after crack. So, it all begins with a good marriage. Love and respect are just what we do to enhance the beauty of our marriage. It is what we express as a result of the good marriage we have and this wonderful life we live produces the love and respect within us.

If couples can understand this analogy, life will be so sweet and easy. Marriage will be so enjoyable and a lot of the difficulties that we experience will be eliminated. Again, I know it may be very difficult for a lot of people to think that the marriage doesn't require work as I have stated in this chapter, but it is the truth that the blessing is there for you to enjoy.

Marriage is there for you to enjoy not for you to endure and labour for. This is the number one reason why a lot of couples get to the stage where they literally get fed up because they've been working and working. They get completely exhausted seeing very little for all their hard work being put into the relationship.

No amount of work that you do can ever add anything to your marriage or to the blessing which you have received from God called marriage. Once our views on love and respect are rightly calibrated, we will find it the easiest of things to express. As a matter of fact, they are not things that we do so to speak but things that we express because marriage comes with all the love and respect that it needs to sustain itself.

This may come to you as a radical view but it is a fact that anything not emanating from you naturally is going take a lifetime of effort to acquire and deliver. As human beings, we are a people of expressions and our lives are an expression of who we really are on the inside. Marriage is no different. Your marriage is an expression of what you hold inside. If you hold your marriage as a burden then all of your experience in life concerning marriage will be burdensome, difficult and hard.

When you embrace marriage as a blessing, believing it to be a blessing and seeing it as a blessing and you walk in that consciousness, it will be easy for you to fully express what you have inside. Your marriage becomes an expression of what your thinking and mindset consist of.

Love and respect may appear hard and difficult because it just is not within you, it is not there mentally hence the difficulty in trying to give what you do not have. The first thing to do is to have it within you by changing your mind-set and perspective and believing with all of your heart that your marriage came with all the love and respect that you will ever need.

CHAPTER 5
Think Leadership

As we mentioned earlier on, marriage is an institution with its structures, processes and rules under which it functions and thrives. Critical to the growth, success and survival of any institution is sound leadership. Leadership is so vital to any organisation and institution that without it, its demise is certain and can be guaranteed. It is for this reason that huge sums are paid for skilled leadership to head corporate organisations. The marital institution is no different and skilled leadership can do to a marriage what good leadership does to some of the most successful companies in the world.

The majority of the crises we see in marriages are issues that border on poor leadership within the marriage. Therefore, the majority of marital problems can be avoided or resolved through effective leadership in the home. In this chapter, we are going to be taking a hard look at leadership and at the man being a leader in the marriage relationship.

The man takes the role of the leader in the home across all cultures around the world and from a scriptural perspective this is the case. As the leader of the home, he is expected to lead and to ensure that the marriage continues to be in a state of bliss. To be a leader is not the same as being a boss. Leadership comes with a lot of responsibilities. It places a demand on all the great qualities that you were born with as a man.

Being a boss requires fear to be able to achieve the goals that the boss wants to achieve. However, being a leader requires voluntarily given respect in order to achieve the goals of the organisation. This is where many men get confused and see themselves as bosses in their homes and cannot understand why the wife will not respect them. The problem here is that fear is extracted through the force of violence while respect can never be extracted from anyone. Respect can only begin as a recognition of leadership.

You can force people to fear you but you can never force anyone to respect you. Through effective leadership a man will command the respect of his wife and children. He also will command their devotion. When a woman finds a man who leads she will be eternally devoted to him. She will stand behind him and pull greatness out of that man.

The vicious cycle of love and respect or the lack of it is the first hurdle a lot of newly married couples face and stumble at. With the wrong mind-set or perspective on this issue, it might be the very thing that sinks the marriage or causes it to be a marriage of difficulty and pain.

As was explained earlier on, the man says "I cannot love my wife because she disrespects me and bruises my ego through her disrespect". The wife says "I cannot respect a man who doesn't love and cherish me."

Again, the man says "how can I love and cherish you when you have used your words and negative attitude to slay the very part of me that makes me a man?" Again, the woman says "it is the lack of love you have for me that irritates me and generates all the negative feelings and attitudes that I demonstrate towards you" and so the vicious cycle continues.

As we come to understand what leadership is from both angles, we will find out that the very things that divide us and cause difficulties in marriages are actually strengths. These are strengths to be embraced and fully exploited for the enjoyment of the marriage. You may be shocked to find out that (i) your differences are the greatest strengths in your marriage; and (ii) through wisdom you can use these differences to your advantage and make them the spice of the marital life that you so desire.

What true leadership is:

1. A leader takes responsibility

The first thing a leader does is to take responsibility. Taking responsibility is how we force out the maturity that is resident inside of us. We must also understand that with the blessing of marriage, comes the ability to lead.

Taking responsibility is all about owning the effective and smooth operational functions of your marriage. It means you embrace the role of taking ownership and I am not talking about owning the marriage. Instead it is about owning the responsibility for the smooth running of it.

Marriage demands of every man this ability to be able to manage the structures and functions. By this, I mean things like communication, finance, romantic relationship, children and all the aspects of the marital relationship.

Taking ownership means identifying potential problems, current problems and even past problems then finding resolutions to these problems regardless of who is or was responsible for generating the problem in the first place. Taking ownership means that whenever there is a failure in any of these functions you willingly spring up to find the solutions to eliminate the problems. To take responsibility means you do not shirk your duties or blame everything on your spouse. Instead, regardless of where the issues may be coming from, you tackle them head-on to ensure they do not stay or find a place in your marriage.

It means being willing to dig deep to get to the bottom of issues so that they can be properly resolved. In this context, there is no room for being emotional or having an emotional attitude to issues. Rather, you rise up to logically deal with issues as you would expect to in the corporate environment.

In advanced societies, one of the disqualifications of anyone intending to seek to occupy any office of leadership is his inability to disassociate his emotions from the decision-making process. Societies are repulsed by leaders who act based on their emotions, insecurities or falsehood. Leaders are expected to deal with issues based on facts.

So, when you find your wife acting in a way that is offensive or not in line with the well-being of the marriage, rather than lash out, threaten or punish, you patiently seek to find out the real reason for her actions or feelings. This requires a great deal of self-restraint. However, having a leadership mind-set makes what would normally be difficult more of an opportunity to deploy your skills.

Taking ownership means you do not misunderstand what is being communicated and easily take things the wrong way. It means you start learning to listen past what you hear to what she is trying to communicate to you. When you own the communication chain, you take responsibility for eradicating the distortion that persistently crop up. It means you find lasting solutions to these issues as you would in any telecommunications network.

The easier option is to get fed up and abandon everything thinking that a different person will have fewer problems for you to deal with. While that may seem to be the case, the truth is that wherever you go, the institution of marriage is attacked relentlessly with these challenges regardless of who you're with. Also, take note that leadership will always be demanded of you by any woman you get married to.

It is virtually impossible for a woman to be with a man that will not lead. It generates an unbelievable amount of frustration within the woman when a man is present and will not rise up to his leadership position. Therefore, it is necessary for every man to quickly learn the ropes of leadership and pursue the wisdom of leadership. In so doing, he will be able to fully exploit the blessing of marriage or whatever institutions he is blessed to lead.

Leadership skills are non-negotiable in life and, without effective leadership, crises will ensue and chaos will be the order of the day. There are so many aspects of the marital life that can be visited in this area - from finances to emotional well-being; to career; to children and even down to the general recreational enjoyment that a marriage needs for it to be healthy. Responsibility lies with the man to ensure that every aspect of the marriage runs smoothly and there are no issues in the chain.

Last word on this: financial leadership is just as important as every aspect of leadership within marriage. A leader should be fully aware of the financial state of the home at any given point in time. He should take absolute responsibility for anticipating the future financial needs of the home. He should also take steps to ensure that difficult times ahead are dealt with or provided for.

Being oblivious of what is going on financially in the home is one of the highest acts of irresponsibility regardless of who earns a higher salary. To take responsibility is not just you being involved and taking actions. It means, you pointing out possible difficulties that may lie ahead and ensuring that there are solutions in place to avoid financial catastrophe.

2. A leader negotiates the destination of the marriage.

In the context of marriage, it is the responsibility of the leader to negotiate the destination of the marriage as well as the journey to get to that destination. A leader cannot afford to allow situations and circumstances to take the marriage adrift to wherever it finds itself and point accusatory fingers. Instead, it should be within him and from him to sit his spouse down and negotiate the common destination, the nature of the journey and how to get to the destination.

A leader must negotiate the type of marriage that both can agree on and can call a success. The role of a leader is to stick to the clearly defined destination and the agreed journey route. The leader is to take down every challenge or opposition to what has been agreed by both sides as a great marriage.

When a leader sits down with his spouse and they both agree on what a beautiful marriage should be, that sets the platform for the marriage. He will find very little resistance whenever he is trying to correct actions or attitudes that threaten the beautiful experience both parties seek for the marriage. He will find it so much easier to resolve differences and issues when marital paradise is projected as what is being protected and guarded as opposed to his personal feelings and ego.

A leader has a responsibility to continually speak of the marriage as paradise in itself. This continuous verbal declaration of the beauty of the marriage creates an atmosphere that makes it difficult for any contrary experience to survive or even exist. He must be the champion of the reality that you are both in a very blessed thing called marriage. Rather than identifying faults here and there, he must be obsessed with the fact that in finding his wife, he has found a good thing and obtained favour from the Lord as the Bible says. If a leader constantly speaks of the destination to which the marriage is headed, this provides motivation for the follower. It creates a vision which is conceived in the heart of the follower.

As a leader, it is your responsibility to continually remind your spouse that this marriage that you are in is a blessing to be enjoyed. In so doing, you will find yourselves together, naturally fighting every deviation from what is the talk of the home.

The more you verbalise the blessing, the more it becomes the reality you experience. This very important aspect of verbal affirmations cannot be overemphasised as in Scripture we know that words create. It is the job of the leader to continually create the future or what is desired.

3. A leader manages the atmosphere

It is a scientifically proven fact that the atmosphere in which workers work, affects their productivity. In a positive work atmosphere, the efficiency of the worker is enhanced. His self-worth and value are enhanced and there is an increase in his love for the job. This, in turn, causes his devotion to the job to be significantly increased.

The famous philosopher Aristotle once said "pleasure in the job puts perfection in the work". An effective leader of an organisation will create the best atmosphere for the workers. This is not just for the efficiency that comes out of it but for the well-being of the workers themselves.

The institution of marriage is no different in this respect. A leader has the responsibility to manage the atmosphere in the home and there are several things that a leader can do to influence the atmosphere of the marriage. In a healthy atmosphere within marriage, there is less friction in dealing with issues and challenges that arise. Taking on this very important function will significantly make all other things easy and the application of other principles smooth. This is not just about making your spouse happy but it is about generating an atmosphere that literally drives the marriage.

Now, it will please you as a leader to know that your marriage came with all it needs to generate that atmosphere. Therefore, it isn't something that you need to go and look for outside - it is already within you. Your job as a leader is to draw out this atmosphere and guard it.

Below are several ways in which you can enhance a positive atmosphere in your home and in your marital relationship:

Constantly verbalise your marriage in a positive light

This is the most powerful atmosphere-creating force – your words. When you use your words to affirm your marriage as being a great marriage regardless of any apparent difficulties that may be present, you create an atmosphere in which difficulties find it hard to survive in.

It cannot be overemphasised the importance of your positive view of your marriage being spoken to and in the hearing of your spouse and even to others. By constantly speaking of your marriage as a great marriage and as a living paradise, you literally demolish any difficulties and starve them of life.

You will find that your wife begins to agree with you over a period of time that your marriage is great. When she starts to believe that, her entire perspective and the way in which she reacts to things in the marriage aligns with the fact that you do have a great marriage and are living in marital paradise. You may just find this impossible to do considering a great deal of bitterness and hurt you feel right now. You might think to yourself that this is just a lie and there's no way I can call a painful marriage any kind of living paradise.

It is important for you to understand that the difficulties that you may be experiencing right now in your marriage are only being sustained by a negative perspective and negative words that are spoken. When you start to speak the right words concerning your marriage you extinguish every atmosphere of negativity in which negative things can survive.

This is exactly how God operates as the Bible tells us, "He calls those things that are not as though they exist" (Romans 4:17). In exactly the same way, you use your mouth to speak into reality whatever you aim to experience.

Even better than that is the fact that the very institution of marriage within which you find yourself is a world of blessings and unrestrained happiness that already exists and you do not need to create. So it isn't a lie but the truth.

It is very difficult, if not impossible, for any woman to fight against or demolish a positive atmosphere that is being consistently reinforced and that produces peace and happiness in both lives. The more consistent you are with your positive affirmation of your marriage the more she gravitates to that reality over a period of time.

Regularly praising your spouse

It cannot be overstated, the impact that gratitude and appreciation have on a person and on what they do. When you make it a duty to praise your wife and thank her for things that she does, regardless of the fact that these are things that she is supposed to do, she immediately recognises the fact that she's not being taken for granted. She will see that she is valued, cherished and her efforts are appreciated. This creates an atmosphere in the marriage where she enjoys doing the things that she does. She will actually go on to do even more because of how you make her feel when she's around you.

Praising her for the way she handles situations, the way she looks and dresses; praising her for being such a good wife and a wonderful mother to your children will make her love coming home and valuing her time with you. This doesn't mean that when issues need to be dealt with or when you disagree with a particular line of action that you cannot speak. No. However, because of the awesome atmosphere you have created and do create on a consistent basis, you find that you are able to correct or advise when necessary without generating a negative reaction.

Showing care and concern

Regardless of whether you can solve an issue or not, just generally enquiring about the potential issues in the home and how they affect your wife creates a wonderful atmosphere. By showing empathy and understanding even when you don't agree with her will go a long way to fully establish an enriching and enabling atmosphere. Being proactive with your care and concern will be far more appreciated than your ability to solve the problems or potential problems that your marriage faces.

Now, negative atmospheres usually evolve out of frustration and resentment that exist within the man or the woman in the marriage. Your willingness to discuss uncomfortable issues or issues of disagreement immediately disarms the feeling of resentment and frustration as each party feels that at least they have been heard. Usually, the resentment doesn't come from being disagreed with, but it proceeds from the frustration of not being heard and understood. Opening these conversations and being willing to show care and love will ensure that you are in a relationship where difficult issues can be dealt with in the most loving atmosphere that you can imagine.

Deliberately taking down words and attitudes that poison the atmosphere

As a leader, you must understand that you are responsible for the atmosphere in your home. This atmosphere will have an effect on everyone including your children and even the visitors that come to visit you. Part of leadership is directly confronting attitudes and words that may potentially poison the atmosphere in your marriage. For example, calling the attention of your spouse to the effect of their words on the well-being of your marital relationship. This also means confronting yourself when you find attitudes and feelings that have the capacity or capability to poison the atmosphere in your relationship. It means exercising control over your mind and making a decision to use the power of self-restraint to stop yourself when you find yourself being the problem.

4. Solving Problems as a Leader

It is important to know that when you take on the leadership position as a man and start solving problems in the marriage or around the home, you'll start becoming a major inspiration to your wife. If you continue on this path long enough she will not only become absolutely devoted to you and love and honour you but she will worship the ground on which you walk. If you notice that you are constantly demanding respect from your wife, it is an indication that she has not been inspired enough by you.

I know this may be very difficult for a lot of men to accept and many of you may say "you do not know my wife, she's the most horrible and nastiest person on the face of the earth. She is rude, disrespectful hot tempered ill-mannered and just generally a nasty person who is completely controlled by her emotions." Even if this were to be the case in your home, this is a simple problem that can be resolved regardless of the background or whatever may be driving her attitude or behavioural actions. How? By simply taking a step back and looking at these issues as problems to be resolved and not to be reacted to. Then, by applying proven problem-solving methodologies you'll soon find out that these are no major issues to contend with but opportunities to sharpen your leadership skills and bring out the king in you.

There are several types of problems in marriages and these include communication problems, financial problems, physical and emotional intimacy problems, recreational problems, health problems and other issues too numerous for us to mention. Whatever the nature of the problem that you face and regardless from where these problems arise, whether from your spouse of from yourself, once you start embracing the mentality of a problem-solver your worth and value in that environment explodes.

Imagine being the father and husband who is greatly loved and adored by your spouse and your children! I am talking about where you are held in such high esteem by your spouse that she sees you as the greatest person ever to walk into her life. You cannot begin to imagine the kind of treatment you will experience in the house.

The key here in being a great problem-solver is to always be able to take a step back and separate your emotions, hold back your reactions and attack problems with the mind-set of a problem-solver. It means you have an end-goal in mind. It is not just solving the problem but going down to its roots and completely annihilating the seed of that problem. In so doing you bring transformation to the life of your spouse in a very positive way. This takes a lifetime to learn but it is a journey you can start and begin today by choosing to apply this approach as often as you can when you are confronted with problems within your marriage.

This deals with any excuses you may have or putting all of the responsibility on your wife. Instead, it puts the responsibility back on you and lets you know that it is in your hands to bring a particular issue to resolution. Always remember that problem-solvers are greatly rewarded in the corporate world and it is no different in marriage.

5. A leader builds and adds value.

One of the great outcomes of effective leadership in any organisation is building people up and adding value to the lives. What does it really mean to build somebody up? To build somebody up includes empowering people to be more than they were before, to do more than they could do before and to live better than they did before. There are things that happen to us as human beings - environmental factors that affect us in ways that tear us down and weaken us in life. Things that negatively affect the quality of the life we live, the way we act, and our ability to come to our full potential.

When a leader takes on the mentality of a builder, it means you identify in the life of your spouse those things that do not project them at their best but causes them to be and act lower than their true potential. Now, it is not just enough to identify areas of weakness but also going the extra mile to use your words and actions to inspire growth and regeneration in the life of your spouse. It means even going out of your way to encourage your spouse to take on projects and things they would otherwise not have the audacity to take on.

When mistakes are made and weaknesses are displayed, rather than react to these mistakes or weaknesses, a leader will stand with his spouse, gently bringing her attention to the issue and immediately begin to speak to the better side of her. An effective leader constantly talks to the queen in his spouse and only deals with her on that level no matter what mistakes are made or weaknesses that are demonstrated.

In building and adding value to his spouse, a leader is constantly lifting her up to such an extent that she gets so used to an exalted life that she no longer knows what it feels like to be down. She no longer knows what it is to behave or act lower than her exalted position in her marriage. She is made to feel like the queen that she really is and in so doing is transformed into that very image in every possible way. Soon enough, the whole world will begin to treat her as the queen that you have made her to be.

Now, in adding value to the life of your spouse as a leader, you tackle this in exactly the same way that you receive value in your life from others. Adding value flows along two streams. The first stream is enabling your wife to do and to be what she would otherwise not have been able to accomplish by herself. The question you must ask yourself is "what would she like to be or do that she is currently finding it difficult to accomplish?" Then you take action to explore every possible action that you can take to empower her to accomplish her desired goals.

The second aspect of adding value to a person's life is primarily focused on the things that you do for that person that makes their life a better experience. The question you must ask yourself is "in what way have I made the life of my spouse better since she got married to me?" Look at this question carefully and if you find yourself wanting then it is time to take action.

6. A leader fights against any threats

Effective leadership includes protection of the marriage and family unit. It means being able to identify potential threats to the marital relationship and dealing with these threats before they strike the marriage. There are several things that will be hurled at your marital relationship to destroy it and take it down. Being an effective leader is being able to identify a threat for what it is, confronting it and taking it down. I will give you a few examples of potential threats to your marriage.

(i)   External relationships that have the potential to negatively affect your relationship. These should be dealt with before they affect the relationship. There are certain friends you or your spouse may have that may not be good for your marriage and these ought to be identified and moved away from. Very close relationships with the opposite sex that may appear to be healthy and harmless at present could have the potential of causing serious problems if not dealt with. When these are identified, effective leadership is calling them exactly what they are and making sure that they go no further in your marital relationship.

(ii) In-Laws and external family relationships. These should also be put in their proper places so that they do not become a threat to your marriage. Being a good leader is being able to manage these very important family relationships which have a very important role to play in your life, the life of your spouse and your children and yet all these have to be skilfully managed through wisdom.

(iii) Inappropriate behaviours and desires. Things which you see cropping up and having the potential to become a significant threat to your marriage must be confronted and dealt with before they become serious problems.

These are just a few examples I have given above concerning potential threats to your marriage but there are an innumerable number of potential threats. However, the real principle here is being able to identify something that you know is not correct in your marriage then rising up and dealing with it as the leader that you are.

The Rewards of Effective Leadership

As we have stated earlier on, marriage is an institution, and like other corporate institutions in this world, effective leadership is critical to its success. We have also stressed that a huge price is always paid for good leaders and when leadership is proven to be effective there are incredible rewards for the leader who has led well. One may ask, how can a leader within the context of marriage be rewarded?

Before we go on to examine the rewards of effective leadership in marriage, it is important to highlight the great responsibility the leader bears in the institution of marriage. Marriage is not for boys, but for men. It takes maturity and a great deal of wisdom to be able to handle a woman in marriage as well as all of her emotions that make her the woman that she is. Being a leader within the marriage demands that you understand what your wife is trying to communicate. It also means understanding the different methods and ways that have been created for her to express herself.

It is important to know that to confidently lead a woman to a desired goal or objective within the marriage requires skill, patience, love, understanding as well as a great deal of respect for her. Yes, I mean a great deal of respect for your wife as this is the minimum requirement to effectively inspire her to a desired place or an agreed objective of the marriage. It isn't because women are difficult people. They are just special and delicately created by God to be special and to be treated as the angels they are.

When you are being effective in taking her into marital paradise then you can begin to enjoy unbelievable rewards for your leadership and we shall examine some of these below:

1. The love and affection of your wife!

It is one thing for a man to love a woman but it is a whole different matter when a woman passionately and deeply loves and adores her man. Naturally, we are very used to men pursuing women, loving them and seeking to have them. However, when a woman is gripped with love for her husband, that man will enjoy things he never knew existed before.

It is important to mention here that women have the capacity to conceive in the place of physical intimacy, to incubate and give birth. When a woman comes to love you as a man because of your leadership function, you will experience emotional intimacy with her. This is where your dreams and your goals in life and all of your abilities and potential are caught (conceived), incubated and delivered on your behalf as a result of emotional intimacy. A woman in love will take a man's pain and turn them into his gain. She will take his fears and make a lion out of him.

When a woman is in love with a man, that man will find a place where he can bare his soul, his greatest fears and his deepest thoughts and be sure to find comfort and solutions in his wife. This is a place that very few men in this world ever get to and the few who ever get there will not trade that place for the whole world.

Most men will use everything they can find from drinking to sports to hanging out with the guys and even having affairs or visits to prostitutes to deal with their vulnerability and numb their desire for emotional intimacy. After all, men are not supposed to show any sign of emotional vulnerability or weakness and when it begins to manifest, they run helter-skelter seeking for what can only be found in the depths of a wife's love.

Only in your wife, and in her alone, can a man really find this satisfaction that he so badly longs for. The average man usually thinks that if you can get more women he will be happier and his desire for intimacy will be satisfied. Were he to pursue this line of thinking he would soon come to find out that the more women you have the more you want and the emptier you feel. It is for that reason that we can firmly conclude that there is only one place where a man can be so completely satisfied that he has absolutely no desire for any other woman in the face of the earth. This is in the depths of his wife's love and affection.

Regardless of the raging sexual drive in a man and the constant lust he has to battle with as a natural born man, there is only one place where this thirst can be quenched once and for all. This is a place where he can finally be free from this uncontrollable desire within him which has the potential to completely ruin his life and that of his family. That place is in the depth of his wife's love. So many lives are wasted in affair after affair, from prostitutes to addictions in the quest to be physically and emotionally satisfied and all the efforts come to nothing. For to look for this satisfaction outside of your wife is like looking for the living amongst the dead.

A wife embodies a secret chamber within her, a nest so to speak where every thirst in a man can be quenched to the point of satisfaction. This place can only be accessed through the deepest part of the woman's love for her husband.

2. The respect and devotion of your wife!

This is one of the biggest rewards of being an effective leader in your marriage because all that makes a man a man, is this thing called ego. This ego must constantly be fed in order for the man to be at his peak and at his best. This ego of a man feeds purely on respect and honour. When this is denied or the opposite is dished out to him that causes his ego to be bruised, his very manhood is under threat. As we stated earlier, there is nothing a man can do to force a woman to respect and honour him, it is something that can only be voluntarily offered. Even if you get the woman to fear you, you can never get her to respect you, for respect and honour proceed out of the depths of her love and admiration for you.

When a man steps up to lead in his marriage, to patiently and skilfully handle his wife and all that she comes with and still bring her into marital paradise, he will stimulate a devotion from within her towards him. Now according to the Bible, the man is instructed to love his wife and the woman is instructed to submit to the husband and these are things that should be done regardless of the other person.

However, when a woman is not acting just merely out of obedience to Scripture but actually acting from a place of inspiration, it becomes easy and enjoyable and addictive for her to honour her husband. She has become so inspired by your leadership that she's swept off her feet and entirely devoted to you and lost in holding you in high esteem, treating you like a king just because you make her feel like the queen that she is. She becomes very creative in honouring you and finds a great deal of pleasure in doing so. It becomes natural for the man to have an expectation within him that whenever he's around his wife he is certain that he will walk away feeling on top of the world.

Respect and honour are a necessity to a man and integral to his masculinity and this is his deepest need in any relationship. Without this he will know no peace neither will he be at his best in life. Regardless of the race and cultural background, the greatest need of a man is respect and honour. When he is disrespected consistently his confidence levels go down and he becomes aggressive or reactive to everything and this puts him in a state of disequilibrium.

A man's ability to perform and excel in life is tied to his ego. A disrespected man or a man who is constantly being dishonoured will never be able to perform in the home as the man that he ought to be. Neither can he excel amongst his peers in life. However, a man that leads at home will be rewarded with the type of respect and honour that causes every latent ability and gifting within him to come into full expression.

3. A world of fewer problems

As stated earlier, leadership is all about responsibility and solving problems. Effective leadership therefore leads to a world of less problems since a majority of these problems would have been attended to.

Indeed, the problems that emanate from unresolved issues will not see the light of day. Usually, the problems that demolish marriages are usually what one would describe as secondary or tertiary problems. These are problems that arise out of the presence of other problems. These are problems that came out of issues that were left unresolved and grew to be huge cancers producing all manner of illnesses in the relationship. An effective problem-solving mechanism in place will save a man a lifetime of stress and difficulty.

With little or no problem, a man's resources will be free to be deployed towards other endeavours and pursuits. He will be free to accomplish a great deal in his lifetime as well as make a significant impact on his world because his mind will be at peace and his focus intact. A problem-free life makes for a very prosperous life in which the entire family can benefit and go on to fully realise their potential.

4. Great leaders create order which in turn increases productivity and efficiency.

The efficiency we speak of here is the smooth and optimal running of the marriage and family life where minimal resources and effort produce maximum benefit. Leadership is all about organisation and utilisation of resources to produce all the things that are to be enjoyed in the marriage.

Effective leadership manages what is invested in the relationship in order to maximise the output of that investment. Here we speak of the production of joy, happiness, memories, emotional well-being, financial stability etc. In the context of a marriage, it means wisely utilising your words of kindness and taking time to do the things that please your wife and not wasting resources on things that do not please her. It means using your reactions positively and effectively managing your time to ensure they are memorable times to be cherished.

It is painful how people pour in so much resources financially, physically and emotionally and yet completely fail to achieve or produce anything of worth just due to the lack of effective leadership. We have often heard women say "I am not interested in your money or the big things you buy for me. I just want you to spend time with me because none of the cars or jewellery or clothes you buy me mean anything to me". Now this is a great tragedy due to ineffective organisation and use of resources in the relationship. Leadership will guarantee you a better quality of life. Leadership will make you spend quality time and not money on gifts when what is needed is love and not material gifts. In the same vein, it will make you buy gifts when that is what is needed instead of you sitting at home and wanting to spend time.

CHAPTER 6

Stirring up the Leader in Your Husband

As stated earlier on, marriage is an institution that needs effective leadership. There is no negotiation about this or a way out concerning leadership in a marriage. It is important, it is critical and an absolute necessity. So, what happens when my husband will not lead and is totally oblivious to his role and function of being a leader in our home and marriage? What do I do when my husband just doesn't know how to lead and take his position? What do I do when my husband is completely obsessed with my faults and abdicates and neglects his leadership role?

It is the responsibility of leaders to solve problems and every problem in a marriage can be solved through wisdom. Likewise, the problem of abdication of the leadership role or the reluctance to lead or the unwillingness to lead can be solved by the follower through wisdom. Yes, it can be extremely frustrating for a woman when the man is not taking on the leadership function in the marriage. Not only can it be frustrating, it can actually be very hurtful and extremely difficult for a woman in a marriage where leadership is an issue. One of the most difficult things that wives experience is the issue of: "how can I respect the man who will not take on his leadership role and function?"

As we stated in the beginning, marriage comes equipped with all that it needs for it to be successful and to be enjoyable. It is just a matter of knowing how to deploy all of the blessings of marriage to make it paradise on earth. Now, the Bible tells us in the book of Ephesians chapter 5, that the man should love his wife and the wife should respect the husband and herein lies the secret weapon with which any woman can solve any problem emanating from the man and his position.

Stirring up the leader in a particular person requires a great deal of wisdom and strategic thinking. There are certain things that can be done not to get him or force him to do leadership things, but for the leader in him to rise up in order to begin to function as he should. There are a few practical keys that unlock the leader in your man. It is important to remember here, whether he is leading or not, the innate leader lies dormant in him.

So, it isn't that we are trying to make him to be that he isn't already, but it is just an issue of awakening the sleeping giant within him. Therefore, the mind-set to have here is not: "let me try and make a leader out of this useless man" but instead "let me wake up the king in the palace."

1. Crown him the King

Every queen needs a king just as every princess needs a prince. If the king in the palace is oblivious of the fact that he is the king or he has been talked down from his throne, then a new coronation or swearing into office can be held for him to mount the throne. This is the very principle that stimulates the leader in a man. Due to several factors, past failures and issues in the marriage most men come to a place where they feel absolutely worthless and powerless in their marriages. They then just find a position of survival and stay there throughout the marriage.

Sometimes it is the shock which a man experiences at the beginning of the marriage where his authority is challenged, his leadership is assaulted and he is disrespected or dishonoured that causes him to dismount from his position and begin to see himself in a different light. It is for this reason that he needs to be crowned a king again and as often as necessary until he settles into that position. And, just before you react negatively to the thought of crowning any human being your king, just remember that you stand to be crowned the queen.

The next question is: "how do I go about crowning him the king of my world or the leader in our home?" Well, exactly as it is done in the natural world which is a very definite procedure, so it is in the marital world. You need to sit down with him so that you can talk to him. In that conversation, regardless of where things are or his behaviour so far, you let him know that you embrace his functional position as a leader in this institution of marriage that you both are in.

In this conversation, in unequivocal terms without any ambiguity you let him know that you accept him as the leader in the marriage and as the king of the home. It is here that you also let him know that you are not in contention for that position neither are you there to challenge his authority. Instead, you 100% embrace him as the leader. This is not the time to bring up past issues where he hasn't acted as a leader or hasn't behaved as the king that he should be.

Rather, you stay focused on the coronation activity that is going on and refuse to be distracted or drawn into past things. You firmly let him know that he was put in your life for a specific reason and you have no qualms with him as the leader of your marital institution. You let him know that, as a matter of fact, you embrace and celebrate him as the leader and apologise for not having seen him as the leader all this while.

I know this may be very difficult for you to take as a wife who is probably frustrated and bitter with your husband who has abdicated his position as the leader in your marriage. However, it is a necessity in order for chaos to come to an end and for peace and order to reign in your marriage. It is important that one sees the wisdom behind this, for where there is no coronation there will never be a king on that throne.

2. Speaking to the king in him

It is a very popular saying that if you talk to the fool in a man the fool in him will come forth. Also, if you speak to the king in him, the royalty in him will come forth. The nature of greatness or leadership or kingship is such that it responds to stimulation and that is why kings are praised and their praises are sung at the entrance.

We do not need psychologists to tell us that words make a great impact on the lives of people. Nor do we need them to tell us or how many people have been completely cut down and imprisoned by demeaning and condescending negative words that were spoken over them or to them at different times of their lives.

It is very natural to see people being talked down so badly to a state of worthlessness, where they actually see themselves as being without any value and trigger the weakest part of humanity in them. This can go on to control their actions and behaviour because of how worthless they believe they are. Just as negative words can destroy people's lives, so can words of royalty build and stimulate the greatness in a man. Regardless of the intention, men will always believe what they keep hearing over a period of time. Additionally, what they believe is what they become and what they become they act out and experience.

When you constantly address the king in your husband or the leader in him, it won't be long. The great dormant leader in him will wake up to the sound of your words and they will begin to saturate every aspect of him. The question to be answered or to be asked today is: "what is your husband hearing from you?" Do you speak to him as a person of importance, of *great* importance for that matter, or do you speak to him without any honour or respect as just an object of frustration? The entity you are speaking to will determine the entity that you will get for there is a way to talk to so-called mere men, and there is a way to talk to kings. When you start to address your husband in the way kings are addressed, the king in him will begin to respond.

There are four important moments in the life of a man where his vulnerability is exposed and you have access to both the greatness in him and the weakness in him. The four moments I speak of are: (i) when he gets it right; (ii) when he gets it wrong;

(iii) when he doesn't know what to do; and (iv) when you argue. It is at these very important moments that your words and the tone of your words make or break the man you have in your life. In the times where he gets it right and achieves some level of success in any particular endeavour, your words to him in such moments should be words of praise. Your words should affirm his identity and position in the relationship and your admiration of him as a leader. This should be said in a way that conveys you see him as being a living embodiment of success and a great leader to follow.

The second most important moment where your husband can truly be reached and the king in him be stirred up is when he gets it wrong, or experiences some kind of failure or just didn't meet an expectation. At such times, rather than talking him down or speaking to the failure in him, it is actually the best time to speak to the leader in him.

Let him know that he is bigger than his current negative experience and that you see him as a true leader with the capability to overcome the impossible. At such times you speak words that lift him up to the throne he ought to be occupying and you continually let him know that you have a great deal of faith in him.

The third important moment when you truly touch the leader in your husband with your words are in times of confusion or seasons of not knowing what to do over a particular issue or situation. In this period, empathise with him. Let him know that you believe in him as a leader and as someone who is responsible for making decisions. Fill his heart with comforting words that consistently point to him as an effective leader whom you have every confidence in. Confusion is torment in itself, and a man is no more exposed than in a season of confusion. Take advantage and unleash life transforming words of affirmations and greatness. Remind him of every time he ever came through difficulty; of your commitment to stay with him through thick and thin and never stop believing in him.

A fourth point to take into account is your words when you argue or disagree or even quarrel. In the heat of an argument, it is very easy to come out with words that slay and hurt as well as dishonour and demean. There is nothing that affects a man more than when he's being challenged or his authority is being belittled. It destroys him.

Therefore, it is very important to take advantage of this moment when you're supposed to be showing disrespect to actually turn it around and use it as an opportunity to build him up just by using wisdom in dealing with him at such moments. In such times, you may say things like "you are the head of the house and I really don't want to be rude to you. However, I do disagree with you on this and I hope you will see my point of view."

By you affirming him in such a situation, it immediately begins to revive the leader in him and once that leader is awake, he will naturally take on his responsibilities and be the leader that he should be. This may be difficult for you to get into but it solves a whole lot of problems and it is the wisdom key with which you access the leader in your husband. Using words such us "I have so much respect for you but...", "I know that I should never speak to you disrespectfully, but right now I'm just so angry" or "it really hurts me every time I have to raise my voice at you to get your attention".

In being able to express yourself and yet lacing your conversations or disagreements with nuggets of respect and honour you stir up the lion in him and the king within begins to come forth. Even for a man who is leading effectively, this strategy is necessary on a regular basis to continually remind him of his position and his authority in the home.Whatever a person continues to hear on a regular basis, he begins to believe and whatever a man believes, that is the life he acts out. Use every opportunity you can find to gracefully speak to the leader in him and the greatness that is hiding within.

Regardless of how frustrating it may be for the woman, when her husband isn't leading it will be completely counter-productive for the woman to go on an offensive against him and belittle him or call into question his leadership ability. To do so is to take a hammer and destroy the very bridge you need to get to the other side. Deploy the weapon of affirmation in order to bring into existence that which did not exist before. Even the Bible tells us that this is exactly how God operates "He calls things that do not exist as though they do" (Romans 4:17).

So, when God finds a defeated man or a weakling, He calls him great and a mighty man of valour. This is a very important principle that you as a woman must master as it is the key to bring into existence that which you currently cannot see in existence but you know is present deep down in your husband.

3. Royal treatment fit for a leader

It is important for us to understand that in order to bring certain things to life, it requires stimulation. An example of this is how a heart that has stopped beating through stimulation can be brought back to life and to beat again. As ridiculous as this may sound, it is the only way to bring back a heart that has stopped beating back to life. Anyone who would want to experience heart revival must submit to this law of stimulation.

Kings respond to palaces and all the royal treatment and honour that comes with the throne they occupy. To be king requires a certain atmosphere that is saturated with homage, praises and exaltation. Without these, it is impossible for any form of authority to be established or function. It is no different in marriage. As soon as the right atmosphere is in place, the sleeping dormant leader will respond from his slumber, even from his frozen state and wake up to be who he was designed to be.

Now, the thought of treating your husband in whom you are currently very disappointed as any form of royalty may cause your blood to boil. Your emotions may be filled with rage but the truth is that wisdom demands this to be the only way to bring a frozen king back to life in order to reign over his kingdom and better the lives of his people. In the same way, in order for the king to emerge, which is what your marriage so badly needs and without which it cannot succeed or be enjoyable, you have no option but to create the atmosphere - not for his sake but for yours. This is great wisdom.

You must see beyond the immediate implications of your

actions and think of the marriage more holistically and act in the interests of the marriage. Therefore, you creating an atmosphere of honour and royal treatment for your husband will only produce one thing and that is a king or a leader.

Now, if you treat your husband as a mere man, or as a servant, then a mere man or a servant will emerge and there's no getting away from this. Natural thinking will tell you that he doesn't deserve any kind of good treatment and that he must first start being an effective leader before he can be treated as such and the whole cycle continues and the impact on both lives is nothing but a living hell. Here the very objective of what we want is lost and the woman loses at the end. However, through wisdom, the original objective can be achieved and the greatest leader that you may ever come across will emerge from taking the right steps.

Let me be clear here by saying that I am not asking for you to make yourself a foot mat to be trampled upon or disrespected. No. We are talking about using wisdom to skilfully achieve or obtain the desired objective. Take practical steps to make him feel like a king. Treat him with respect and not just any other man but the most important man in your life who deserves the greatest honour you can ever give to any man.

Treat him better than you treat your boss at work or your pastor in the church and hold him in the highest esteem. Even if it is obvious that he doesn't deserve it, you will be amazed at what will come out of your actions. In whatever ways you engage him, do it with an extra level of excellence, whether it be in the way in which you speak to him, raise issues with him or handle disagreements with him, let it be fully saturated with respect and honour. Even down to daily practical things, which in the past you may have overlooked or both parties are comfortable with, such us choosing to serve his food at the table or doing something just to show honour and respect in whatever way that works for you and effectively communicates the value you place on him.

All effort must be put forth to secure an effective leader for your institution of marriage, for without this the marriage is destined to fail and the experience a living hell.

It is important that one sees the wisdom at work here. It is said that "a person can handle any 'what' if only they knew the 'why.'" When you understand why your husband should be treated as a king in an atmosphere of royalty, it will be easy for you to do whatever it takes to create this atmosphere and to make him feel like the king he truly is. What is at stake here is not just the success of the marriage but its survival and smooth functioning. You may disagree and say "I just cannot bring myself to treat this worthless man as a king, I would rather dump him and go find me another man who's going to rise up to his leadership position." The truth is that life is filled with challenges and wherever you go and whoever you're with you will always have challenges to be overcome.

These challenges will present themselves in different ways but, at the end of the day, you will still require wisdom to overcome the challenges that await you. We were built to dominate our world and to subdue it and not run away from it. Therefore, it is important that we rise up to the challenge and use the resources and knowledge at our disposal to overcome these challenges.

If only you can see the greatness in the man in whom you have married and the potentials that lie within him, you'll come to find out that the effort required in stirring up the greatness in him is nothing to be compared to all the benefits his leadership will bring to your life and marriage.

4. Deliberately letting him lead

As we have established earlier on, leadership might require stimulation for it to come alive. One of the ways in which leadership is stimulated is by actually allowing your husband to lead by deliberately taking a step back and allowing him to face situations that will force him to make decisions. Even though some of these decisions may be wrong you must let him find out so that he develops his decision-making ability. Certain things that you would ordinarily handle by yourself, you can take these things to him and let him make a decision or provide leadership just so that you can stir up the leader in him.

It means getting out of the way, taking a more relaxed approach to things, especially those things that are inconsequential. It is okay for people to make a few mistakes in order to learn and it is no different with the husband who's been stimulated to lead. Continually take issues to him for resolution regardless of his attitude towards them and it will only be a matter of time that he begins to rise up to meet the expectation you have created of him.

Sometimes people are forced to lead when followers appear and demand leadership to a desired destination. It is exactly the same with the husband who is not leading. A lot of the things the wife will usually bother herself with which should be handled by the husband must be handed back to the husband and ensured it is followed through under his leadership.

An important aspect of this is bringing the decision-making process to him because leadership begins with taking responsibility and making decisions. So, if the leadership in him must be stirred up, it will require that on a regular basis you have enough decisions on his table to work on no matter how trivial they may be as this will cause him to respond to the value this places on him. This will cause him to start to see himself in a different light of importance which in turn will stimulate a change in attitude to issues and challenges that come against the marriage. By constantly bringing the decision-making process to his world or desk, you cultivate the skill that he will need to lead.

5. Praising him for instances where he led

As we stated earlier on, kings require the traditional pomp and praise singing from time to time in order for him to function and lead. It is exactly the same way for husbands. Make sure you take the time to constantly acknowledge everywhere and every time he has shown leadership and to praise him for it. Express how proud you are and privileged to have him as your husband.

No matter how small or minute the issue is which he dealt with, unleash on him words of recognition, words of affirmation and words of celebration. By continuing to magnify little acts of leadership on his part you unconsciously generate higher levels of expectation from him and he involuntarily finds himself acting towards the expectations on him.

CHAPTER 7

Stirring up the Queen in your Wife!

A husband may be screaming "help - my wife is not acting as the queen that she is, she has a very nasty attitude, she's aggressive and explodes in fits of anger and rage which doesn't just leave me embarrassed but completely broken as a man." It may be a situation where the wife has zero respect and honour for the man and treats him with little or no regard.

It may be a situation where the wife is totally oblivious to her role as a wife in keeping a clean and orderly home as well as ensuring everyone is well-fed and nourished. It may be a wife who is inconsiderate and just spends way beyond her means dragging the whole family constantly into debt or it may be the wife who just doesn't care whether the marriage survives or breaks down as long as she has her own way unchallenged.

Whatever the scenario may be, the truth is that within every woman is a queen in waiting that can be stirred up through wisdom and understanding. No matter how outrageous her behaviour and attitude may be, the beautiful gracious and elegant lady is without a doubt present within her. Accepting this truth is the beginning of a life of joy and happiness for you as a husband.

It has been commonly said that a woman is like a rough diamond that is discovered by a man. The man has the responsibility to bring out the sparkle and the beauty in that rough diamond. Without sounding condescending, just as the jeweller has the responsibility to polish a rough diamond until every beauty and brilliance begins to shine forth so it is with every man and his wife. It is the responsibility of the man to continually add value and bring out the best in his wife for the best is truly buried in her somewhere and the patient man will discover internal beauty beyond words.

In this chapter, we will stick with the rough diamond analogy and the man's responsibility to polish this diamond until no further beauty can be found or expressed. Again I stress that viewing a woman you have just met as a rough diamond does not in any way make her any less of a person or incomplete as a human being who needs polishing. Instead, it puts the focus on the latent beauty and brilliance that goes beyond the surface.

When we begin to change our thinking along these lines, and look beyond the actions and reactions of our wives so that we may touch the very rare gem within, we bring forth the object of inestimable value that is within her. This is when to you and in your eyes your wife becomes nothing short of an object of incomprehensible beauty and value. Such a view of her triggers this beautiful one who by nature continually expresses an altogether loveliness that pleases the soul of a man.

It is important to state here that we are not trying to get the wife to behave in a certain way or have a certain attitude for that is a futile mission. Rather, we are awakening the beautiful one who, without any effort but by nature, expresses such beauty and brilliance in every way in which she carries herself and deals with her man. Again I stress this point, trying to force your wife to change is an endeavour destined for futility that will do nothing but irritate her and intensify the very behaviour you are trying to change. In turn, this will make your life a living hell. Instead, she looks for the man who can bring the best out of her. Below we will look at practical ways in which a man can bring forth the beautiful one whom we speak about or what we would call the Proverbs 31 woman.

1. Crown her your queen!

What does it mean to crown a woman your queen? In very practical terms, it means deliberately making her the most important person in your life no matter how hard this may be. Now, as a husband you may say "this woman has wounded me so much and is currently the very object of my misery and sorrow. To make her the most important person in my life will be to enthrone my pain and sorrow." However, if you hold on to the mind-set of a diamond polisher you will be able to have in focus a real gem and see past all external behaviour and actions in order that you might lay hold of the priceless beauty within.

Crowning her the queen of your life is the first step in realising the wonderful woman that is buried within her. To crown her your queen is to establish, and effectively communicate to her, that she is of immense value to you regardless of external behavioural issues and that you are fully aware of her worth and value. When you think about the crown on a queen's head, what immediately springs to mind is beauty and value and this is what you must verbalise on a very consistent basis.

Never stop talking about the value and worth of the diamond that is within, looking beyond what is being portrayed on the outside and it is only a matter of a very short time that every external aspect of her life begins to conform to the inner beauty that is greater and excels in brilliance and beauty. As it is with human nature, when a person consistently hears a particular thing, they will start to believe and act accordingly.

It is painful to watch how men have walked away from women of priceless value just because they could not recognise the hidden gem in the wife they had married - just because the externals did not look like what they had expected. It is like a miner who throws the world's biggest diamond away just because he couldn't see past the dirty state of the diamond ore.

It is common knowledge that when diamonds are discovered they look nothing like the polished product and have no brilliance nor clarity. In fact, they can be easily confused as some stone of no value at all. It is very easy to view your wife as nothing but trouble or as a decision which you regret based on the difficult times you may be experiencing in your marriage. However, with wisdom, understanding and a little patience, you can get past any negative external attributes and mine out the diamond that is within her. You will then find out that you cannot begin to put in figures the value that is buried in the wife that you have married. It is very easy to judge people based on external circumstances but it takes a special eye called "wisdom" to see past the external stuff and take hold of the valuable person within. Like we said earlier, crowning her the queen is communicating to her in words and actions the value you discovered in her.

2. Exalting her with your words!

Like a ritual, a husband has the responsibility to constantly speak words that lift up his wife - not just words of affirmation but words of exaltation. Here we are talking about words that lift a person higher than their current physical position whatever that position maybe. It's about not been trapped in the current situation and circumstances or attitudes of your wife but constantly speaking about the potentials within as if they were already being demonstrated in her.

There are two levels of exaltation and the first one is ensuring that you identify her current abilities and acknowledge before her these abilities, praising her for them as if she was the only person in this world to have them. It means appreciating the good things that you see or encounter in her and accentuating her strongest points or what we call her strengths. It even goes further in taking the time to get her so intoxicated with everything that is good about her that she starts to lose awareness of her weaknesses and failures. In doing this, you are able to correctly handle mistakes that she makes or attitudes that may be wrong without damaging the person to whom you are married.

Without this understanding, attempts to deal with issues will end up becoming theatres of attack because of sheer frustration. When you verbalise her strengths way more than anything else in the marriage you find out that there is hardly any room for words that put down, hurt or inflict wounds that debase the value that a wife may begin to feel about herself.

The second level of exaltation is speaking to her potentials and her future. This is a very powerful tool in the hand of a husband to stir up the queen in his wife. When you continually speak of things that your wife, in reality, may not have attained or be in possession of as if she is already in possession of those qualities, you trigger a reaching for those heights within her.

Remember that the force within a person that responds to spoken words is unstoppable. By words, you can motivate people to achieve the impossible. Knowing how to use your words on your wife is a very vital and necessary skill in building up the wife that you are after.

All of humanity seeks to be around people who build up and not the ones who break them down. The reason being that it is an established fact that words add so much value to the lives of people to the degree that they are able to produce what they would ordinarily not have been able to produce.

An important aspect of speaking to the potentials within your wife is that you create within her a mind-set of success and a "can-do" attitude. You unconsciously put within her a nature that knows no defeat. You create within her self-confidence and I cannot overstate the value of confidence within a person.

3. Love her and her brilliance will come forth!

Sticking with our diamond analogy, the value that is resident in your wife is priceless. It is all a man could ever dream of with abilities that exceed your imagination. Even the Bible tells us in the book of Proverbs 18:22 "Whosoever finds a wife finds a good thing and obtains favour from the Lord". This is so because in your wife is a gem of inestimable value. Earlier on we talked about the fact that the beauty, worth and value of a diamond is not immediately visible at the point of discovery. A diamond requires the art of diamond polishing for all of its brilliance, beauty and work to come forth.

In exactly the same way, at the point of discovery of your wife or at the point of marriage, all that you see and encounter is only a tip of the iceberg. It is only an external coating that hides an unbelievable gem on the inside. Because diamond is the hardest material on earth, besides all the tools that will be used, the jeweller will need to use diamond to polish a rough diamond and this is how diamonds come forth in the jeweller's world.

However, in marriage, in order to polish this rough diamond that is buried in every wife, she will need the strongest force on the face of the earth and that is love. This is because love can cut through anything that it encounters and file away every undesirable outer coating.

So powerful is love that it is able to completely bring out every beauty, every brilliance and every sparkle that is locked inside of that diamond and bring out the true value of the diamond itself.

It is vitally important that a man understands there is no other way to deal with that which is locked in a woman except through the power of unconditional love. Mastering the art of using love as a weapon and as a tool to polish off every negative attitude, every nature of rudeness and disrespect will guarantee any man the finished product of a woman of substance.

Love is both the raw material and the process itself that brings out the queen in any wife. The love that we speak about here is not the love that you feel but the love that you do. It is the love that rests upon a decision made, a love that understands its purpose and a love that never is deceived or bows to external ugliness.

Lastly, it is important to mention here that there must be a mind-set change with regards to the view you have of your wife. View this as new information you have received about your wife which should cause your perspective of her to change. A man must see through and see past all external reactions whether good or bad and get right to the woman of substance that is within. You must get to the woman who will make your marital life a living paradise here on earth, the woman who will make you experience levels of happiness and joy that you never knew existed before. While people are different, the process is the same for every woman and it requires the same great deal of patience, skill and recognition of value in your wife.

4. Cherish and adore her!

The evidence of value that is perceived in anything is in how it is cherished, adored and protected. The degree to which you recognise and comprehend the value in your wife is the degree to which you will cherish her. The advice here is not so much to cherish her as to think and recognise the value in her that automatically causes you to cherish and adore her.

The more you saturate your mind with positive things about your wife, her capabilities and potentials, the more you will find yourself cherishing her and holding her in high esteem. The temptation to focus on external attitudes may be very strong but the truth is, to do that is to deliberately allow yourself to be deceived and lied to. It requires a firm determination to not be moved by external experiences but focus on the one of immense value within, a stand which will bring positive transformation into the queen she was born to be.

Women respond to being treated as special, priceless and valued. The woman of substance in her will come alive as a husband begins to cherish and adore his wife. The marriage moves from a dimension of "doing" to one of "being" where she acts because "she is" not because it was demanded from her.

CHAPTER 8
Returning to base

With all that has been discussed so far, for any marriage where one partner embraces these truths, significant undeniable changes will begin to be experienced in the marriage. However, the question really is then how do we move forward from here and what will the experience be? How will this new reality be held together and what about challenges when they come? We will look at a few points below.

1. A new nature, a new reality!

The minute something clicks inside of you and you begin to see your marriage in a completely brand-new way you will know for a fact that you have entered into the reality of what has been discussed so far. Further proof of entering this new reality is when you begin to watch the negative perspectives you once had concerning marriage melt away. Instead, all of a sudden, you will experience a refreshing within and have hope regarding your marriage. Where marriage was once viewed as an impossibility, now you see it as such a simple life to be enjoyed and no longer a life of pain and misery. Yes, that is when you know for a fact that you have touched the new reality.

Reality is something that you cannot deny. Due to the fact that you are in a new enlightened world concerning marriage you will find out that there is a newness to your marital life. This a place where strife and difficulty find it impossible to survive or stay. The dawning of this new reality creates an atmosphere and a feeling within you of marital bliss - even before things begin to change physically in your marriage.

Regardless of which of the spouses embraces this truth, the impact is felt. There is a peace that settles into the home that causes arguments and fights to become foreign to your relationship.

In maintaining this new reality, the only responsibility one has is to stay in the consciousness of the truth you have learnt earlier on. There are two key facts you need to focus on to maintain this new reality: (i) the fact that marriage is good; and (ii) the fact that you live in marital paradise. Let these facts saturate every aspect of your being to the point where this is what comes out of you when you are hit with anything regarding your marriage. This becomes the sole platform from which you respond to your spouse or even deal with your spouse. It becomes the glass through which you view and interpret the actions, even the mistakes, of your spouse.

The only way to stay within the consciousness of anything is to give yourself entirely to that thing and in this case the words written in this book that may have changed your marriage. Identify the key truths that have impacted you and read them over and over and over again so that they find a place in you and become a part of you.

Consciousness is a function of focus and whatever you focus on you become conscious of. Therefore, decisions will have to be made regarding what will be focused on in the marriage. Will I focus on mistakes, weaknesses or hurts or will I set my gaze on this whole thing called marital paradise? This is a question that will need to be resolved in every heart and mind as whatever you focus on, you become conscious of and it becomes a reality.

2. Elastic – The new normal!

Something else that you should expect to see in your marriage is a wonderful phenomena which I call the elastic marriage. This is very straightforward. It means that no matter how far the marriage departs from the state of marital paradise, with very little or no effort it finds itself back in that state of peace and joy. It becomes elastic in nature and when pulled by circumstances or issues that pop up, no matter how severe they are, the marriage just finds a way back to its original state of marital bliss as opposed to a state of growing bitterness.

It may be that you have a spouse who would like to test to the limits your so-called new found revelation on marital bliss yet, no matter what is thrown at it, the marriage returns itself back to equilibrium. Marital paradise becomes the base and bedrock of your marriage. The marriage itself finds it difficult to depart from this state because of your grasp of the consciousness that marriage is a blessing.

So powerful is this reality that it subdues and dominates every other reality that attempts to rear its ugly head. This is because the blessing is of a higher dimension and superior to every other natural reality. Forgiving your spouse becomes not just easy but natural to you. Resolving issues becomes second nature as difficult and knotted issues are easily unravelled due to the presence of this light which is the truth that marriage **is** a blessing.

3. Handling challenges when things flare up!

As human beings it is very normal for us to sometimes react and flare up. Just when you think marital paradise has become the reality in your marriage then you experience a situation that causes anger to be expressed either by you or by your spouse. Then you begin to question whether you really are living in marital bliss. The wisdom here is not to look at flare ups as being a confirmation that there is no such thing as marital paradise for you and your spouse. No. Neither is it confirmation that marriage will always be difficult because of the person to whom you are married. Rather, you are to see these flare-ups as opportunities to deploy the wisdom you have received.

Issues and challenges are only opportunities for you to give expression to the reality of marital bliss and its ability to dominate and overcome whatever comes its way. These are opportunities to allow what is in you, what you have acquired via divine wisdom to find expression in dealing with and handling matters relating to your relationship. Issues popping up are nothing to be scared of or surrendered to. Instead, see these issues as the degree to which more wisdom is needed in that particular area.

Everything that is built will certainly be tested either by natural elements or by supernatural forces. When you take a stand concerning your marriage devilish forces will rise against you and try to pull down what you have and reduce you to a lower level of thinking and operating. This must be resisted fiercely and you must hold on to the fact that your marriage is a blessing and not a curse. Be resolute and determined to enjoy your marriage and turn it around whenever it goes off course.

The way to handle what I call flare ups, which are not necessarily issues, is by always taking a step back in the heat of the moment and reacting from a place of knowledge rather than feelings. When things are being said that hurt your feelings or irritate you, as you react put at the forefront of your mind that this is the spouse who you consider a blessing and who you share a life of marital paradise with. It is something that is perfected with some practice! When you walk and operate from a place of knowledge, you get on top of situations and exert control over the atmosphere in your marital life.

CHAPTER 9

Putting All this Together

Up to this moment, so much has been said with regards to marital paradise, especially the different components that make marital bliss a reality. With all that has been taught, especially in the area of changing one's mindset on marriage, the big question that comes up is "how do I put all this together to bring my marriage into marital paradise?" There are five different components that answer this big question of how to put all this together. We will look at them in detail below.

1. Will the sun ever shine over us again?

Your relationship may have gone through an unimaginable amount of sorrow, pain and heartache not to mention the public embarrassments and the fact that everyone is aware of the type of marriage you have been living in. There is probably so much animosity between you and your spouse, and even so much hatred for all that your spouse may have put you through. For the fact that it has gone on for such a long time causes you to ask the question, can the sun ever shine into such darkness?

The good news is that light itself, by nature, is built to completely extinguish darkness to the point where you no longer see it or experience it as the light shines brighter and brighter. This is the very purpose of the light, to completely extinguish the darkness that exists.

The light of this truth that is entering into your mind concerning your marriage is in itself able to light up your world to the extent that you will begin to doubt if you were ever in any marital crisis. Regardless of the gravity and the enormity of the difficulty of your marital experience of the past few years, this change in mind-set will give full expression to the truth that lies inside of you.

I have seen the most difficult of marriages so completely turned around that no one will ever believe that this couple have ever argued with each other throughout the entire marriage. The more difficult and bad the marriage may have been the greater the turnaround when one's thinking is changed.

Anyone receiving this truth must believe without a shadow of doubt that their marriage will come into a world of bliss. Be fully persuaded about the truth that your marriage is a blessing; that marriage in general is a blessing from God.

Believe with all your heart that through divine wisdom you can fully exploit all of the blessings that are available to you. As long as you set this truth in front of you that marriage is nothing but a blessing from God, a living paradise on earth and a world of absolute enjoyment, the light of this truth will illuminate your world and the sun will shine again on your marriage.

2. How do we deal with past hurts?

So much may have happened and a great deal of hurt and wounding may have accumulated over a long period of time. In such circumstances, one or both spouses may not have the will nor the strength to take any more steps forward due to the sheer exhaustion the relationship has brought you to. This pain in the heart is felt on a daily basis and is deeply rooted in regret. Many have wished they could just take a pill to stop the heart from hurting. However deep the hurts maybe, the only way out of this imprisonment is for truth to enter in to that heart.

A popular verse of Scripture from the Bible says, "and you shall know the truth and the truth shall make you free" in John 8:32. When you are illuminated with divine truth, it brings freedom from darkness, freedom from the imprisonment of marital distress and freedom from the lie that marriage is hard work. This great lie that marriage is difficult has been singularly responsible for the very difficult experiences that a lot of people have had in marriage. If one can get over this issue and have their mind changed about marriage eradicating every thought that marriage is hard then, in that same second, every hurt and pain within will be evacuated. It will be so completely removed that you will soon forget the days and years of pain and sorrow. The earth only experiences darkness when it turns its back on the sun but as long as it sets its gaze in the direction of the sun, it must receive light and that light gives life to the planet. It is exactly the same marriage wise.

This is the quickest and most effective way to get rid of emotional hurt and pain. It is mind-set transformation when divine truth enters. Here we are talking about an evacuation of every deep-seated pain, total annihilation of those feelings of regret and instead experiencing a peace and hope for tomorrow. You will be so amazed at the instantaneous extinguishing of the pain in the heart due to the entrance of divine truth.

3. How do I sell this to my spouse?

In this chapter, we have invariably used the analogy of truth and light in the context of experiencing a change. If we stay with this analogy and build on it, then it becomes immediately clear that there is no responsibility to convince your spouse or win them over to this truth that your marriage is a blessing and a world of bliss. All you need to do is to allow this light to shine. As you begin to walk in the light of this truth and operate in the reality of marital paradise, the first thing that will happen is that you will find true happiness and joy within you. It will only be a matter of time and I mean a short time before your spouse catches on and settles into your world of marital bliss.

All it takes for marital change to occur is for one person's mind to be illuminated with the truth about marriage. The spouse, along with everything else, will fall in place. So you need not worry about convincing your spouse or selling this to him or her. All you need to focus on is being fully persuaded that marriage is a blessing and a world of unending happiness.

Your spouse will know for a fact that something has happened yet can't quite put his or her finger on it. This does not mean that you shouldn't have a conversation about what you have read in this book. By all means. please share everything you have picked up with him/her and if possible get them to read the book as well. As for you, what you must do is stay focused on the truth and never take your eyes away from them and your world will change.

When you take on what you have read and begin to live it, the first thing that happens is a change in the atmosphere, regardless of the behaviour of your spouse. I say this because you have been elevated by knowledge or shall we say the light of the truth. You are able to operate from a higher dimension of life and to exercise and exert greater control over your immediate environment. You find yourself not being entangled by the little things that used to trip you up and keep you in an atmosphere of strife and emotional hurts. Seeing from a higher perspective, you are able to deal with your spouse beyond the outer expression and will instead get to the depths of the heart seeing the root cause of the behaviour. When you are able to deal with and resolve issues on a heart level, you are far more empowered to change external behaviour by correcting heart defects. By this, I mean misconceptions, anger, misconstrued emotions and incorrect assumptions can be corrected which will in turn change a person's thinking and in turn the behaviour.

You can see here, that it is not a question of you convincing your spouse. It is a question of you operating in the level of knowledge that you have within you. Because you are so saturated with the truth and reality that marriage is a blessing, you find yourself with great ease not doing anything that perpetuates the lie that marriage is difficult or is meant to be full of strife and pain.

You find yourself not reacting in shock to things but being able to handle issues as they come. It is like discovering that you are a far more better person than you've always thought of yourself and just being your new self. This here is not calling for you to become a foot mat to be walked over but instead to have the added advantage of being able to see down to the smallest component of things. Divine wisdom breaks things down to the smallest nuts and bolts where you can see where things have gone wrong or are due to go wrong. You can apply fixes to them as opposed to being totally confused and overwhelmed because things are not broken down into smaller components.

There is no one who comes in contact with light and prefers darkness where they are limited by little or no visibility stumbling over things that should be enjoyed. When your spouse sees a total change in your view and approach to marriage and your ability to differentiate what is to be reacted to and what is to be understood, they will marvel at this great power within you and will yearn for it with all of their heart.

What we are talking about here is not even demanding that you change but it is demanding that you change your thinking and perspective of marriage and of your spouse.

A changed mind will change the way you feel when things are done to you that you would have significantly reacted to in the past not knowing the reasons for which they were done or the place from which such actions came out of.

In summary of this point, on how to convince your wife or husband of marital bliss, it is important to mention that nagging or forcing them to read this book or forcing them to change will be counter-productive.

What you must do is give full expression to what you have learnt, regardless of the side of the fence which you are and let what you know dominate your behaviour and thinking completely. You will see how easy it is to get your spouse hooked on marital paradise. Continually verbalise in the house the fact that you have an awesome marriage and a great spouse. Declare how easy marital bliss is and in no time you will have your spouse and their friends walking in the same marital enjoyment which will rule your home.

3. How does all this become my reality?

As was mentioned earlier on, it isn't really a matter of waiting for your spouse to change, the only change here that is relevant is your thinking and the marriage itself. I say this because a marriage that has been based so many years on untruths and a lack of divine wisdom will certainly be in a very dark and difficult place. By reason of you coming in contact with the truth about your marriage as an institution, not only does your mind-set change, but the marriage itself experiences a change by exiting the place of darkness and deception and entering into a place of light.

As you continue to speak of your marriage in the light of what you have read and believed and how you consider your marriage to be an awesome blessing to your life, you will find your spouse will start to change their mind-set too. This in turn will radically change their behaviour and how they act. One of the things about wisdom is that it puts you in charge of any particular situation or circumstance and in this case your marriage. When you are in charge, you are positioned to effect the necessary change for your marriage to experience a fresh awakening of joy and peace.

It is important to remember here that people are primarily governed by their thinking and mind-set and they only act out and experience who they are on the inside. Now, with you having your mind renewed you can expect to see changes in your attitude and behaviour towards your spouse

4. Make a decision to be happy in yourself!

The majority of people enter into marriage with the mind-set of finding somebody to make them happy. There is nothing that could be further from the truth because no one can make you happy. Happiness is something that must come from deep within which you can give expression to.

Obviously, I say this with the caveat, knowing fully well that there are things that people can do for you that cause you to feel good and have momentary feelings of happiness. However, the happiness that stays whether anything happens externally or not is the happiness that can only be found deep within you. You cannot hand over your happiness to anyone nor allow anyone, not even your spouse, to determine whether or not you are going to be happy.

When this truth is assimilated you will find out that the things that used to ruin your day no longer have the power to do so. This is because you have taken control of your happiness or, better still, you have started looking at the right place for the source of your happiness. This is a very important aspect of marriage to be understood and grasped.

Being fully in charge of your happiness means you can determine not to get into unnecessary fights in your marriage that do nothing but drain you and your resources and achieves nothing other than to set you back. In this position, regardless of how much you are goaded when your spouse is spoiling for a fight you steadfastly hold your position and refuse to get into a fight especially for things that are inconsequential.

Being able to master this art of refusing to fight an unnecessary fight will save you a lifetime of stress and sorrow. When you make a decision to be happy and to live happy you are able to overlook things and weigh them in comparison to the value of you being happy.

Entrenching your position in this decision to be happy you see the power of self-control over things that you attempted to do to bring happiness to your spouse, yourself or to your marriage. You are able to control what you decide to do or decide to leave out of your marriage. You also control the drama that you will permit from external people be they in-laws or your own family members or even friends. A decision to be happy empowers you to be able to nip in the bud negative attitudes from people who do not respect your space or the atmosphere in which you live and that includes your spouse.

A decision to be happy makes you into a peace-maker as well as a custodian of the peace. Rather than allowing little arguments and disagreements to turn into huge mountains, you find yourself being quick to resolve things and not letting them get out of hand or go any further than they should go.

Making a decision to be happy empowers you to be able to understand issues down to its roots and intentions as opposed to being reactive to the things that come your way from your spouse. Because you live in a state of happiness, you find yourself thinking before acting or reacting and in so doing you live a lifetime without allowing anyone to put you down or make you sad.

CHAPTER 10
The most important person in your life!

After all is said and done, the greatest discovery in your marriage will be the realisation that your spouse is the most important person in your life regardless of the health of your relationship. As long as you are married to your spouse, they will forever be the most important person in your life. Until this is embraced, understood and accepted, there will be a lot of difficulties in the marriage. In this chapter, we will explore in greater details what it really means for somebody to be the most important person in your life and how you can significantly benefit from that knowledge.

The importance of your spouse is not derived from their behaviour or attitude but actually from the position that they occupy in being your spouse. The importance we speak of here is a positional importance and its significance cannot be overstated. So, it is not a question of how can this wicked wife or husband of mine be the most important person in my life? How can the person whom I have so little regard for or the one that has caused me so much hurt be the most important person in my life? The truth is by reason of their position in your life they have the ability to significantly influence your experience here on earth.

Wisdom is being able to quickly recognise the importance of your spouse and begin to treat them in the light of the importance and position that they occupy. Understanding this very important aspect of marital life is key to getting the best out of your spouse. This is the cry of every single spouse, for their partner to understand and accept their importance in their lives and treat and deal with them accordingly. A firm grasp of this reality will solve the majority of the difficulties that people experience in their marriages.

Again, I will say it very bluntly, your spouse is the most important person in your life! It is one thing to know this and a whole different matter to accept it and actually make him or her the most important person in your life. It is something that has to be done and it is one piece of truth that you need to put before your eyes on a daily basis and remind yourself.

What does it mean for somebody to be the most important person in your life? How do I make my spouse the most important person in my life? In order to be able to make this a reality, there are certain key components that must be in place and when these things are set up everything else will naturally flow and you will find that spouse of yours truly the most important person in your life. Below are the key components that shall be discussed.

1. They are of significance to your life!

When you make it a deliberate decision to award significance to your spouse in your life, it means that you are consenting to the fact that they are worthy of attention and play a major role in your life. To be worthy of attention in this context has to do with the fact that their presence in your life is so major that they are taken into consideration with regards to decision-making, planning, personal desires, goals and the general atmosphere in which you desire to live. Here we are talking about recognising how vital they are to how you live and experience your life daily

This significance must be clearly communicated as it comes with responsibility on their part. On the whole, it confers on them a sense of value and worth in the relationship. This also affects their confidence in the home as well as outside.

This is a very important aspect of the home life where we can find the confidence we need to win against the challenges outside. The spouse must know that they are important and are a significant aspect of your life. If that can be effectively communicated to them, their whole attitude will change. They will handle you with so much care and love that it will solve a thousand problems even before they pop-up.

2..They are of great value!

To make your spouse the most important person in your life, it is important that you open your eyes wide to see the hidden values and capabilities in him or her and celebrate them. In any human being it is whatever you go looking for that you will find. If you set out to look for the great things in your spouse you will definitely find them. You must let your spouse know that there is more to them than meets the eye and that they are so much more than they exhibit on the outside.

Your spouse should constantly be mystified about the value you perceive in them which they are yet to see. It is when you have searched for the good in your spouse that you can confidently say "I see so much in you".

When you calibrate your mind with regards to the value of your spouse, it will affect how you treat them, how you respond to them, how you handle their opinions and how you deal with their weaknesses. This issue of value is so important in the marital relationship that, until it is dealt with, there will always be problems in the marriage.

Value determines the price one is willing to pay. In marriage, value determines what you are willing to give and to do for your spouse. Until the value issue is resolved in your thinking, no matter the intentions, you will never be able to rightly handle your spouse in the way he or she should be handled.

In life, the things that are of great value are handled with the most care. The truth of the matter is that your spouse is of more value than anyone else on earth and should be handled with a great deal of thought and care in line with the value of who they are. It is also a fact of life that whatever you belittle or trivialise you will eventually lose. So, it is important that you work on your mind until it is settled within you that your spouse becomes the most important person in your life.

3. They are a necessity

It is fundamental human nature to be wanted and it is important that your spouse has this feeling and knowing in them. To make your spouse the most important person in your life you must clearly establish the fact that they are not just wanted but they are actually needed in your life. It means communicating the fact that you cannot imagine life without them even with all the challenges you face in your marital relationship, the good still outweighs the bad. You'll be amazed the impact that this has on a person's behaviour and attitude. This helps us to understand that the outward you is usually controlled by the inward. So if we speak to the inward person and deposit thoughts of greatness within, then there will be an outward expression of positive attitudes.

Through wisdom a great deal of calamity can be avoided in life. So many things that are broken can be repaired to the benefit of all and it is exactly the case in marriage. Certain actions that may look very foolish can avert a great deal of problems. For example, even when you feel like you're fed up with your spouse, let them know that in spite of everything they matter in your life. By doing this, you will be able to rebuild to perfection things that have been broken down over the years in your relationship.

4. They are the priority of your life!

An important aspect of making your spouse the most important person in your life is by making them the priority. It means they are before all others, before everything else, and above everyone else. In simple terms this means you do not treat anyone better than you treat your spouse or place anyone higher than them. It means establishing a culture where you do not permit any competition in any way when it comes to your spouse but you instantly place them first before others in all things.

For example, before you praise anyone's wife, you ensure that you have praised your wife so much that she doesn't even care about you praising somebody else's wife for the way they behave or conduct themselves. Another example is that you never ever exalt any man or speak highly of any man in terms of their capabilities in any way that makes your husband feel less of a man.

If anybody is going to be getting any praise, let it first of all be your spouse. Also, in the area of opinions, it means you value their opinion more than any other person's. It means you take into consideration their feelings and advice above all others. There are several examples we could go through however the long and short of it is that your spouse is to be fully confident that in any situation they are first in your view and are treated as such.

Secondly it is important that it is established that your spouse is above all other things. By this, I mean that he or she has first place over your hobbies, your work, your friends and your material possessions. When you place your spouse above issues you find that those issues disappear along with the atmosphere for competition which generates dissent and strife.

It is great wisdom to eliminate and protect your spouse from all forms of competition in your marriage. In this manner, energy can be used for more productive activities in your relationship as opposed to retaliating or trying to deal with the anger that arises from being put in second place. This applies to both men and women in marital relationship.

Thirdly, in order to make your spouse take their rightful

position as the most important person in your life, you place them above everyone else. In most cultures, it is very important to respect elders and in-laws and to seek advice when necessary. However, it is important to establish that in your marriage your spouse is above all others when it comes to how you deal with issues and plan towards the future.

This does not in any way encourage disrespect towards important people in your lives. As a matter of fact, when your spouse is occupying the right position in the marriage, you will find out that they naturally become very respectful to the people that are important to you. Again, this issue of competition that generates hatred and strife is eliminated.

Your spouse should have the confidence that in the home, no external voice is valued higher than theirs and that no one is treated with more love and respect than him or her. It is important that marriages have people that have been entrusted with the power to speak or correct things that may be wrong in the marriage. However it is also very important that after all is said and done externally, the voice of your spouse matters a great deal.

5. They have influence based on position.

It is important that your spouse knows that they have the capacity and the power to influence things in the home. It is important that in the marriage, they have a voice that is heard. It is your responsibility to also communicate to them that their influence in the marriage is not based on their behaviour or how much money they bring into the home. Rather, their influence is based on their position by virtue of being married to you. By deliberately allowing your spouse to exercise reasonable influence over some of the decisions that you make, you give a great sense of importance.

Regardless of the stronger personality in the marriage, when your spouse knows that they have the ability or the capacity to influence the direction of things in the marriage, you create more of a team partnership which will be of great benefit to the marriage.

The most important of all!

In this book, we have focused squarely on marriage and how to come into marital paradise but of greater significance is the purpose for which you are here on earth. Without purpose, life is meaningless and empty. As a living entity, there is a purpose to your life here on earth beyond survival and eventual death.

The primary purpose of your creation and existence is to be a part of God's family, to be in a relationship with Him and to live with him forever. Your life here on earth is only a staging ground and an opportunity to be saved and redeemed into God's family.

The entrance of sin into the human race, caused it to become defective and in contradiction to the nature of God who is the source of life. As a result, the human race became separated from God and separated from life. Humanity came under the condemnation of God and doomed to destruction due to the absence of everlasting life.

God, in His great love, has sent His son Jesus Christ to save humanity from this condemnation and to restore it back into the family of God, to give everlasting life and the forgiveness of sins.

Until a person receives this new life, one's existence here on earth will not really have any meaning or make any sense. Also until you receive the gift of the forgiveness of sins, there is a certain condemnation that hangs over us all the days of our lives!

Today you can receive Christ into your life and have all of your sins forgiven and your life fully restored to a glorious way of living.

To accept this wonderful gift of salvation from God all you have to do is believe with your heart and confess with your mouth your acceptance of His Son Jesus Christ as the saviour of your soul. To receive this salvation, you can pray this prayer and you will be instantly reborn into the family of God:

Dear Lord Jesus,

I believe with my heart that you are the Son of God and you died to save me from my sins.

I accept you as my Lord and saviour and ask you to come and live in me.

I receive the gift of salvation and the forgiveness of all my sins.

According to your word, I am saved and born anew into God's family.

In Jesus name!

If you have just prayed this prayer, then you are born again and have just received the gift of eternal life and this life is a present day reality in you. Please look for a bible believing church in your city and begin to attend services so you can learn more about your new life in the family of God.

Also please do get in touch with us and let us know that you have made this decision and we will do all we can to help you in your walk with the Lord!

THE MARRIAGE CLUB
Bringing you into marital paradise

The marriage club is not just an organisation but a vision! It is a vision to see couples experience their marriage like it was the best thing that ever happened to them.

The Marriage Club is a movement with the objective of spreading Godly wisdom amongst the married that produces unimaginable marital bliss. It is also a movement that equips and prepares the singles for a life of marital bliss. It also aims to make it easy for single folks to meet and connect and enter into married life with ease!

This vision is being pursued through various events that are planned like black-tie dinner events, marriage coffee evenings and cruise getaway holiday packages where couples are exposed to mind changing truths about marriages!

Lastly the marriage club seeks to establish a culture of Godly marriages and true happiness in marital relationships. When a culture is learned and established, it becomes a way of life! Marital joy can be a way of life for you!

To find out more about the marriage club and how you can become a member, please visit us online
@ www.maritalparadise.com.